More Advance Praise for *Prayers of a Heretic*

A hiss. An incantation. Fevered kisses. The heretical. In *Prayers of a Heretic*, Yermiyahu Ahron Taub sings of the daily, domestic, of the fleshy and the mortal. Listen to these words—dirge, meditation, celebration. Through them, Taub brings us closer to being human and to the divine.
  — **Julie R. Enszer**, author of *Handmade Love*

Piety has a bad name these days. But in these lyrical wrestlings with the flesh and the spirit, Yermiyahu Ahron Taub reminds us that the pious are often the most passionate, and the heretics often the most holy.
  — **Dr. Jay Michaelson**, author of *Another Word for Sky: Poems*

Prayers of a Heretic chronicles the physical and spiritual dimensions on which life itself depends. In a word: shelter. When observed by a poet with Taub's skill and generosity, the acts of seeking, erecting and sustaining shelter become memorably praiseworthy. Readers will be moved by much in this collection, including the sleeping homeless woman in the library "who surely traversed the city in storm and sun"; and the unnamed schoolchildren, "united by navy blue knee socks," carefully educated at a religious school ("the palace of certainty shielding the unknowable"). We aver what Taub avers: "there is no time assigned for prayer the sanctuary never closes."
  — **Kevin Simmonds**, author of *Mad for Meat*

Prayers of a Heretic: Poems
תפֿילות פֿון אַן אַפּיקורס: לידער

Yermiyahu Ahron Taub
ירמיהו אַהרן טאַוב

Plain View Press, Austin, TX

Copyright © 2013 Yermiyahu Ahron Taub. All rights reserved under International and Pan-American Copyright Conventions. No part of this book may be reproduced or distributed in any form or by any means, or stored in a data base or retrieval system, without written permission from the author. All rights, including electronic, are reserved by the author and publisher.

ISBN: 978-1-891386-01-5
Library of Congress Control Number: 2013940154

Cover art "Portrait N14" by Félix Hemme
    with permission of the artist
Cover design by Pam Knight

    Although some of these poems draw upon elements of lived experience, none should be seen as strictly autobiographical or biographical.
    The transliteration of Hebrew and Yiddish in this book follows the American Library Association/Library of Congress (ALA/LC) system.

Plain View Press   3800 N. Lamar, Suite 730-260
http://plainviewpress.net   Austin, TX 78756

Acknowledgments

I am grateful to the editors of the publications, in which these poems, sometimes in different form, appeared or are scheduled to appear.

"J. Edgar Song" (Yiddish) in *Afn shvel*, Winter/Spring 2013; "Thorns Of Perhaps" in *Association of Jewish Libraries Reviews*, September/October 2012; "Ephemera" and "How the Peeping Tom Came To Remember" in *Avatar Review*, Summer 2012; "J. Edgar Song" (English) in *Beltway Poetry Quarterly*, Summer 2012; "Breakfast In the Basement (With Bureaucrats)," "Odessa," and "On Being a Minorities Poet" in *Dead Snakes*, April 8, 2013; "Flotsam Without Jetsam" and "Semi-Somnia" in *The Hamilton Stone Review*, Fall 2011; "Early Talkie" in *Jewrotica*, February 12, 2013; "His Favorite Patron," "Two Sisters," and "Yermiyahu the Book Peddler" in *Misfits' Miscellany*, February 19, 2012, March 2, 2012, and February 8, 2012; "Empty Nesters" in *Poetry Pacific*, Spring 2013; "Dialectic in Abeyance," "A Meditation on the Question of Agency," and "The People of the Book ... Without Books?" in *Pyrokinection*, May 24, 2013; "Cataclysm in Hebrew Class, or, How Yermiyahu First Went Astray," "In Musical Limbo(s)," and "Questions in a Jewish Cemetery" (English) in *Queens College Journal of Jewish Studies*, Spring 2012; "Birdwatching Without Binoculars" and "Pied Piper on Holiday" in *This Assignment Is So Gay: LGBTIQ Poets on the Art of Teaching*, Sibling Rivalry Press, 2013; "Eavesdropping," "Prayers, in Dialogic Embrace," "Staged Reading," and "The Woman Who Did Not Turn Her Sorrow Into Art" in *Toasted Cheese Literary Journal*, June 2012; and "Regina's Requiem for a Friend" (Yiddish) in *Yerosholaimer Almanakh*, 2014.

"Eavesdropping" was nominated for a Best of the Net Award and a Pushcart Prize by the editors of *Toasted Cheese Literary Journal*.

"Yermiyahu the Book Peddler" was nominated for a Best of the Net Award by Philip Vermaas, curator of *Misfits' Miscellany*.

Sheva Zucker graciously proofread all of the Yiddish that appears in the book and provided insightful feedback.

Truly the ideal collaborator, Pam Knight of Plain View Press deftly guided the manuscript to publication.

I am grateful to the following individuals for fellowship and support: Angelika Bammer, Anne Becker, Andrew W.M. Beierle, Zackary Sholem Berger, Ann Brener, Sarah Browning, Regie Cabico, Ellen Cassedy, Julie R. Enszer, Jim Feldman and Natalie Wexler, Krysia Fisher, Ken Giese, Pearl Gluck, Miriam Isaacs, Cecile Kuznitz, Jeff Mann, Erin McGonigle, Jay Michaelson, Christopher Murray, Roberta Newman, Abigail Padou, Peggy Pearlstein, Jenny Price, Eve Rifkah, Kim Roberts, Yankl Salant, Paul Edward

Schaper, Daniel Scheide, Ruth L. Schwartz, Naomi Seidman, Jeffrey Shandler, Gregg Shapiro, Breena Siegel, Kevin Simmonds, Dan Vera, Sheva Zucker, and my sister, Rachel Berman.

Some of my earliest memories of Laura S. Levitt are from the group of nonconformists and rabble-rousers that congregated regularly in the Dobbs University Center (DUC) of Emory University more than twenty years ago. Then and henceforth I have benefited from Laura's camaraderie, generosity, and acumen. Laura has helped so many of us craft an entree into traditions, interrogate and claim our identity/ies, hone our voices, and set down our words. *Always write.* This book is for Laura Laura.

In honor of Laura Levitt,
friend, teacher, feminist scholar extraordinaire

Contents

I. Visits and Visitations

Flotsam Without Jetsam	13
Odessa	15
Two Sisters	17
In the City of Cubes and Cubicles	19
Staged Reading	21
Gift, Unseen	23
What Was Obscured There	25
The Woman Who Did Not Turn Her Sorrow Into Art	27
Prayers, in Dialogic Embrace	29
His Favorite Patron	31
Dr. K., in the Cross-Cultural Institute	33
Pied Piper on Holiday	34
Grace Note, in White and Gold	36
Questions in a Jewish Cemetery	38
Regina's Requiem for a Friend	44
Crossing the Big Box Store Parking Lot	48
Temporary Outcasts	50
Black and White (and Green) and Red All Over	51
Breakfast in the Basement (with Bureaucrats)	53
Bacchanal at Empire's End	55
The People of the Book … Without Books?	57
Bystanders	59
Empty Nesters	61
At Rachel's Tomb	62
The Imminent Arrival of Gleaners	64

II. In the Gleaning

To the Formica Gardens	69
Yermiyahu the Book Peddler	70
Semi-Somnia	72
Mirage	73
Cataclysm in Hebrew Class, or, How Yermiyahu First Went Astray	74

Safety Net	76
In the MRI Machine	78
Pleasure Palace, 1988	80
Ephemera	82
Streaker in Stasis	83
Travels in Brooklyn After Midnight	84
Ex-Boyfriends (with Others), Sixteen Years On	86
On How the Other Half Lived	88
Bisexuality (of Sorts), or, Rabbinical Compromise Unearthed	90
Early Talkie	91
Utopia	92
Trains Passing in the Railroad Apartment	93
Day of Unrest	95
Lush	97
Birdwatching Without Binoculars	99
Disgrace, Ongoing	101
Secrets of Anaïs	103
In Musical Limbo(s)	105
Editor's Edict, or, Bowed by Absence	108
On Being a Minorities Poet	109
Proofreading, or, You Could Just Hire Someone for This Part, You Know	111
Eavesdropping	113
Luddite's Exhortation	115
How the Peeping Tom Came to Remember	117
Fingers Beneath the Gavel	118
A Meditation on the Question of Agency	120
The Spectacle of Spinoza's Specs	122
Thorns of Perhaps	123
Dialectic in Abeyance	125
The Dirty Laundry Poem	127
Credo	128
Way Stations Along the Via Dolorosa	130
J. Edgar Song	136
Beach Glass Necklace	138
About the Author	139

I. Visits and Visitations

Flotsam Without Jetsam

All that I love is marginal, she declared.
I still remember her face at the utterance of those words,
the set of her jaw scattering the *tsatsiki* light—
how we all raced to disagree, eager to reassure,
only to be met by her scorn.
You see, no matter the cause, she had always been there.
Every march since ...,
every strike since ... well, no one really knew.
It was she who had always done the reading,
even if she had never been asked to lead the discussion.
She made connections between texts, between texts and contexts,
between word and deed, word and word, deed and deed,
links that left us gasping, famished, devastated.

But she had never been one to acknowledge the numbers of things,
even as others yammered on about "attendance" and "crowds."
She was not a theorist above the fray;
she simply saw no point in counting.
So what could she possibly have meant by *"marginal"*?
Perhaps it was her mother tongue, whose sounds
made some giggle, others shudder,
and about which everyone had an opinion,
although few bothered to master or even learn it.
Perhaps it was her religion, or lack thereof,
in this land of piety and thunder and stones cast,
her insistence upon the known and knowable.
Perhaps she meant us,
the ragtag dependables who trickled to the scenes of injustice,
who tramped across bridges and banged fists against steel and stone,
who met in unheated cellars on folding chairs
arranged in circles to ponder and mobilize.

She merely fled our gathering that evening,
never explaining herself then or later.
For a while, we continued to call on her, in two's and three's,
climbing in vain the three flights of walk-up,
to the fragrance of cabbage soup and the sonata of bawling infants.
Later, our banners flapping in the wind,
we were left to consider her whereabouts, to wonder
whether she still favored flan,
discordant verse,
dusk glittering over the green lake next to her ancestral dacha.
Handcuffs around our wrists,
we exchanged sensations of our one long-ago picnic out there—
the clarity of the cream,
the bedlam of the raspberry wine,
the light of birch shadows in her eyes,
her curls skirting the heavens' embrace.

It was only one midnight, years later, as I slithered along the docks,
in pursuit of specter, ecstasy ephemeral,
that I stumbled upon her.
Or rather, she sprang out at me
from behind a column,
where I had been expecting, craving another, others.
I wish I could say
whether her spectacles sparkled under the streetlamp,
whether she was carrying a notebook of words at play,
whether her body still bore the imprint of our era in resistance.
I wish I could say that a kind of precision had been attained.
But I cannot.
I only remember her words, half hiss, half incantation:
You with your stevedores; I with mine.
This cannot end well for either of us, you know.

Odessa

Your father wanted to call you
after his maiden aunt Milkah Pesl,
who entered the home one evening without fanfare
(after his mother ran off with that good-for-nothing
to caper under the big top) and stayed
to bathe and feed and heed and teach him his letters
and a way of being good in the world,
while his father sat in the rocking chair by the window,
never rocking, rarely rising, simply staring
at the drawn drapes as if his wife
were hiding coquettishly in their folds.

Only I would have none of it, not because of his aunt,
who I remember chiefly for her taciturnity,
her lips pursed and her bosom, disquieting in its unsentimentality.
Rather, I insisted on naming you, our long-awaited cherub,
after the city beyond dream,
with its melange of architectural marvels,
cultures in confabulation,
the poets composing on national and other themes,
who honed their craft in its garrets and cafés,
the artists who strolled down its stairs
long before film history was forged there,

the city where the future of our people
was re-imagined in parlors and salons.
A revolution has to begin somewhere, as you have learned.
Has there ever been such ardor?
Even now, after the rupture, beneath the coat of kitsch,
you can still see traces of it.
Know that this will ever be your essence.
You have the tools to orchestrate the sublime into fruition.

Tell your father that Milkah Pesl would have come to understand,
Tell him our family might yet be whole
if he could only see. Tell him this, Odessa my love.

Two Sisters

Having helped her sister prepare for a rendezvous with a suitor,
one among many dashing such,
quashing her unease over his beauty and their lack of chaperone,
Having selected for her dearest the gray frock and the rose shawl
and the bonnie bonnet, hours of hawing and hemming (literally),
coaxing and cajoling,

Until finally here, this silence,
although all of that was pleasurable too in a way,
she freely admits.
Well, this almost-silence,
for she can hear the delirium of their father,
long confined to his mysterious sickbed.

Having prepared the meals for tomorrow, checking again the icebox
for the cold cuts and salad, yes they are there, yes they will be enough,
Having set aside their father's medicines per the doctor's orders,
although secretly she wonders how matters would stand
if there were another doctor in town ...
The word "charlatan" flits through her mind; she's seen her share.

Having removed the work dress, hue rendered indeterminate
from months, then years,
of cooking and scrubbing and sweeping and best-forgotten activities,
Having donned the ironed white camisole, as if virginal,
with its flowered lace collar
salvaged from her mother's sewing box still in the attic,

Until she sits before the mirrored stand also once their mother's
and applies the array of creams to her still unlined face,
inhaling their scents—peach, pomegranate, persimmon (of all things)—
the gifts of the orchards that dispel the carriage just departed
in which a man's large hands are now stealing her sister's body
and the absence of hands over her own,

Until she stretches in bed and opens the novel of manners,
Having abandoned the novels favored (at least until tonight) by her sister,
Until she scrawls notes for her reading group on the protagonist's pluck,
Having revived from options waned (market crash, beau gone amuck),
Until she tickles its spine, clasps it against her breast, then closes its
doors against the illustration of a fate so different from her own.

In the City of Cubes and Cubicles

She remembers when she clad herself in a certain way
how she perused the shops on side streets for clothes once worn
training her eye long before there were television shows
devoted to this art examining labels yes but also drape and fit
the potential for longevity but more for color and print and flair

how she was most she strolling down the avenue in spring
the aroma of toast coffee and eggs (with Tabasco or some such)
greeting her and the eyes of arms-folded men assessing her
the winks of earlier inhabitants of these polka dots skipping
ushering her to the temporary part-time curatorial gig uptown

She remembers when words gushed
not for lack of care or discipline
but for the pleasure of trying them on to feel their roll and swirl
as they exited her mouth to feel their ricochet off the posters
and sconces of the hole-in-the wall watering hole

where the new zine was only being imagined how words could electrify
how she could be heard and yet need not worry about perpetuity
since language was malleable who was thinking about stone
for tomorrow would bring other questions equally intriguing ... or not
but no matter since Zoë was so brilliant and the light so smoky

But now she is here still counting her steps in the labyrinth
where words are parsed measured and weighed not for delight
but for efficiency and against the potential for reprisal with the specter
of officials in black robes looming words like record and document
and paper trail and memorandum that make her tremble

when exiting the cubicle just two down and yet
she is fortunate to be here to have this work in this vast room
when so many others have nothing and when so many rail against it
want to end it point to her and others like her as lazy and complacent
feeding off the people as if parasites she is never unaware of this

and she knows that she cannot replicate what was
and must accept where she is now
in the city-state lined with marble monuments and glass cubes
and she is eminently sensible reasonable even
for she is a servant of the citizens and knows the fragility of their favor

and yet she hears melodies drifting out of alleys
accordions and violins evoking steppes and cobblestones and gas lamps
rising out of piss and banana peels and broken glass and rot
the riot of indecipherable tongues and some very fancy footwork indeed
how could she possibly abandon these sounds

and she returns to the ordered chambers of her humility
with the frocks (that still fit) from which she cannot bear to part and
the shoes o the shoes having relinquished the gaze of men in doorways
and to the plastic desk where verbiage is hammered into pallor
and to the moon whose mercy caresses her fevered kisses

Staged Reading

She responded to the ad at a friend's suggestion,
albeit with reluctance.
It had been decades since she had spoken the language,
longer still since reading it.
She had not been the most attentive of after-school students,
as her mother used to remind her, in an institution not unlike this one.
Dredging was the only verb for all of this, she thought.

She made no effort to disguise her concern to the coordinator,
who only pooh-poohed her.
It's like riding a bike, she chuckled grimly.
And then with greater candor: *Besides, it's able bodies we need here*.
The corridors, painted in beiges and taupes, failed to
mitigate the occupants in various stages of disintegration.

Nor could the games the game shows the flowers the orderlies in pastels
muffle the walkers the canes and buzz of the hearing aids
the televisions too loud the pills almost forgotten the wigs askew.
The paraphernalia of the past-prime, the din of near-death, she shivered.
She placed her hand on the door knob to his room.
How ought his role be named? Charge? Listener? Readee?

He sat in a wheelchair by the window, wisps of hair fluttering
over dark glasses, wearing a gray oxford shirt
and black dress slacks, a whiff of aftershave hovering.
Someone had taken care. After introductions, she opened
the volume (from the right side), the letters neither exotic nor familiar.
Dreading a tumult of emotion, she had not prepared for the reading.

And yet the words tumbled forth, the vowels providing signage.
She chose a classic monologue about a ne'er-do-well husband and
his wife long-suffering, given to juicy invective. A way of life closing.
Sometimes he would interrupt, or rather, call out along with the text,
as if her reading simply confirmed what he already knew
and had always known these many years, only waiting for someone,

for her specifically, this no-longer young woman in tweeds,
to render it spoken. When she looked up, or came to, night had arrived.
His head did not droop; his eyes smiled.
She blushed at his compliments on her reading, at his gratitude
gushed. *If only my students ...* flitted through her mind.
Jittery now, she leaned into his left ear, peppered with black hair.
À tout à l'heure, she whispered, *of course there will be a next time*.

Gift, Unseen

He came to her from summer rain, the deluge relentless.
His clothes clung to him
in all the right places, in all the right ways.
As if in a wet dream, she giggled inwardly.
Only she could not see any of this.

She was waiting for him on her knees, blindfolded as arranged,
her chemise organized in disarray around her.
As he disrobed, she inhaled his scents fused with those of the rain and
of her gardens, highlighted in magazines, toured annually by neighbors,
notably her hibiscus, which she nurtured with such élan.

(She remembered how the features editor and the photographer,
with her assistant,
descended for a day,
with their gadgets and lights and wires so tangled,
and still failed to capture its wonder.)

She knew this body, his body, so profoundly
that her not-seeing proved no impediment,
but only served to heighten her need,
as he had predicted.
Everything was proceeding on course.

She could run her hands over the swell of his chest,
through the patterns of hair,
marveling at its profusion so rare for those in his profession.
He allowed this expedition of hands.
This too was part of the agreement.

It was only when she reached his sex,
her body shivering at its attention,
that he placed her hands at her side
and carried her, still unseeing,
to her widow's canopy bed.

Under his bulk strategically positioned, alongside the Shrine of the
Colonel As If Just Departed and the Sons Who Never Call,
her breasts regained their spring,
her veins, always so prominent, receded,
her hair shimmered in bridal luxuriance.

On this charivari night, as trumpets sang out between palm fronds,
as revelers danced in abandon,
as children scattered blossoms on cobblestones,
there will be no money left on the end table, he whispered,
Ours will be this night. Ours will be this night.

What Was Obscured There

Their features are uncannily similar,
almost identical, in fact:
aquiline nose,
high cheekbones,
porcelain figurine skin, green eyes.
Not to mention a form that
virtually no man or woman could resist.
The specifics need not be delineated here,
although suffice it to say that superlatives such as
"comely" and "fine" and "hourglass" and "statuesque"
all come readily to mind.

And yet with such comparable assets, two fates so utterly different.
Lila dazzles the red carpet, festooned with jewels and gowns fresh from
the most daring houses of fashion. In an era when the paparazzi are on
24-hour alert, she guards her remoteness with Dobermans and barbed
wire and alarms and still is always the center of the most
intriguing projects. Occasionally, picture-perfect pictures—the
husband rugged, the girls angelic, the fire roaring—are released.
Reference is made to a castle or something similar near
the Irish moors, although no precise location is ever disclosed.
Even with her husband's arms around her, she shudders in sleep,
certain that she hears the cameras clicking through the rustling of pines.

Lola resists the spotlight altogether. Not that there aren't opportunities
for public commendation, albeit of a different, less broadcast
sort, of course. Still she wants no part in any of that. She keeps a low
profile in a studio apartment in a transitional but "safe" part of
town. If anyone asks, and few do, she has stock answers.
She has mastered the art of vagueness.
Kerchiefs, glasses, vintage clothes can work wonders,
she has discovered over the years. Deflect and disguise is her principal
motto. If men accost her in even the broadest light of day, as they

often do, Lola is ready. Catcalls, lewd gestures, groping, or worse—
seemingly none of it has proven problematic.

Sound on mute, towel nearby, their resemblance came to him suddenly,
although he must have known all along, like
everyone else. He stopped what he was doing,
what he often did at this hour. The stickiness of his solitude.
Some research was in order,
for he really did so admire them both. He knew all of their films.
And he managed to learn quite a bit, rather quickly even.
Both kept their first names, both had graduate degrees,
both had supportive parents.
Or at least so it was claimed.
One never really knows about that, he thought.

He decided to place their images side by side
on the computer screen luminous in his rented room.
Zooming in, he detected the slightest smudging
of Lola's features, as if her eyes and nose had been applied
just a bit too quickly. Really one had to look ever so closely.
Could that bit of carelessness have determined a fate?
Or was it simply the difference in a single vowel in their names?
Was that enough? Of course there had to be more to it than either
or both of these factors, he thought, sinking further into fandom gone
haywire, the quagmire of conjecture and projection,
before returning to the immediate task at (and in) hand.

The Woman Who Did Not Turn Her Sorrow Into Art

You won't find her in a music video,
in grainy black and white,
walking down the river bank,
neo-Gothic national palaces opposite,
raising her forgiveness heavenwards
in a glorious soprano.

You won't find her at an open mike,
or at a closed one for that matter,
spewing her fury scrawled on a notepad
or roiled on a smartphone,
safe, however momentarily,
in the solace of those who'd been there.

You won't find her in a black box theater
regaling the assembled with vignettes
on being spurned carefully spun,
with an uplifting end so as not to deflate,
costumes magically changed,
color and shadow slicing despair into Technicolor shards.

Here she is instead:
on the window sill of her garret lodgings
retracing the path of his fingers nimble with her buttons,
sauntering over her nipples,
her breasts remembering pleasure in its initial,
most essential incarnation.

Here she is instead:
with a friend considering this frock and that—
apple green for a summer picnic in an orchard of any kind,
midnight blue for an evening with a (true) gentleman—
at the mirror of the cosmetics counter, dabbing with discernment,
networks of blue confetti around eyes green and deserted.

Here she is the last time we see her:
curled up in a ball on the floor,
racked with sobs,
snot pooling on the floor boards,
her father's warning her to dare not return
lashing her belly just beginning to swell.

Prayers, in Dialogic Embrace

I.

Let his gifts deliver him
from these cinderblock rooms
in this concrete tower
high above grounds
littered with needles
and those whispering their wares in daylight
whom I alongside others have tried to no avail to eradicate

Let him steer his gifts clear of
certain women whether of night or of day
with their curves and temptation
the pleasure fleeting
and of men salivating who will approach him
with trifles and certainties that never materialize
leaving him slumped in front of the early afternoon television

Let his body in its glory truly a temple rippling and massive
so hard it is to find clothes that fit
that I have fed with chicken and salads not easy to come by here
yet still so fragile for all its might
be shielded on the field from the stomp of metal the pull of hands
the collision of bodies just as disciplined and the snap of bone
the tear of sinew the impairment of mind irreparable

Let him enter rooms lined with books
after and before the ball has been thrown and carried
find meaning in the words that move over the page and screen
in labor that is quiet and demanding in another way
that I have never experienced for reasons beyond this prayer
but whose riches I see even as others refuse so to do.
Do not forsake him, O Lord, for on Your earth, he is all I have.

II.

Let my body deliver us
to where she can walk without fear
of her groceries being stolen
pears rolling bruised out of reach
or her purse snatched for purchase of junk
Satan's powdery redemption
delivered on a carpet of glass shards

Let me not fall into the snare of those
who seek only glitter and escape through flesh
who see not my heart's tentative steps
into the forest primeval
of those who hope to trip me up
with numbers extravagant and words misleading
leaving me locked in a not-even-crawl-space before my time

Let this body sprung somehow from her own in middle age
nourished and sheltered with wisdom I did not always honor
be so adept that she need no longer bend to tend
granite counters and marble tiles and mahogany planks
those ungiving surfaces so unforgiving of bones and joints
and the soft ones too equally terrible the silk nightie and
lace panties tossed aside on unmade beds for her to handle

Let me forge a path to rooms barred alas to so many
with bindings black and brown and red gilded in solemnity
my eyes agile over pages under green light
into a rapture small just right so that she shall be rescued at last
from the snake oil salesmen with their coffered prophecies
so that we may seek Your word together, O Lord,
in the arbor of Eden's delighted gardens.

His Favorite Patron

She came every morning a half hour after opening, her punctuality
breathtakingly reliable if only we took the time to admire.
Only there were materials piled high, particularly from
prolific, bearded men in black and white, calling our attention.
And queries from those hunting for traces of antecedents,
desperate for evidence, any scrap anywhere
of the couple photographed so long ago in front
of the painted backdrop of French doors and silk portieres.

The squeak of her shopping cart wheels heralded her arrival.
A halo of body-unwashed-for-weeks odor shone all around.
Her hair hung down in limp strands,
often covered by a wool hat even in heat.
Her body was wrapped in rags and bags and blankets and coats
of indeterminate hue so caked in matter were they. Even in penning
this ode, it is impossible to sanitize the physicality of the filth.
There was a monumentality to her entrance. That had to be granted.

She set up station at the same spot by a long wooden table,
retrieved an encyclopedia volume from the shelf and fell, smiling,
into a sleep at once profound and buoyant.
How he marveled at that sleep, he who tossed and thrashed
and stared slack-jawed at infomercials late into night.
What was the secret of her successful rest,
she who surely traversed the city, in storm and sun,
in search of the means of survival, he wondered.

Perhaps it was the fact of her body on this chair in the biblio-light.
Hours and positions may be subject to budget nips and tucks,
but the institution would stay. Did she know this,
did this provide serenity from the chaos of the outside.
Or perhaps there was no chaos outside at all, perhaps there
was simply a path, a creativity sculpted from budgetlessness,

honed these many years. And yet why here?
He never asked her any of these questions. He only knew this:

of all the rooms in this marble palace of knowledge,
resplendent with hand-painted angels and roses,
constructed to dazzle in an era when learning was venerated,
she came to this one, to the one devoted to the writings
of a tiny nation hounded over the millennia, whose citizens
were happiest apparently with book in hand and plume on hand.
Of all the rooms, she came to ours.
We gave her shelter. Here she found home.

Dr. K., in the Cross-Cultural Institute

He shuffles along the halls,
the subject of speculation,
the object of scrutiny.
No one bothers to whisper,
given his advanced years.
Some say ninety-three, others, as high as ninety-seven.

His plaid jackets and polyester ties are
long out of fashion (if ever they were in) and frayed from use.
His odor evokes attics and medicine and t.v. dinners.
Not dapper obviously, but dignified, a jarring contrast
to the sweatpants and dayjamas favored by certain co-workers.
The eyes in the stacks cannot turn away.

The technology revolution has passed him utterly by.
Basic computer usage escapes him, a maze of missed cues.
Some contend he hasn't worked in years;
his head is often found drooping over journals few can decipher.
At last he has retired, however reluctantly,
forced to do so, quivering, by the powers-that-be.

Only he cannot restrain himself from this citadel of erudition.
He returns daily, drawn by a force beyond hearsay.
His gait is slower now, aided by a cane.
How does he navigate the buses and the subway, we wonder,
the crush of souls racing to the designer sneaker sale
or the first autumn date in the wine bar with limited seating.

They say he is an expert in romantic poetry,
endowed with insight into image and structure once thought elusive.
We imagine him strolling long ago in the parks of his homeland,
now bedeviled by the faith police and their battalions of thugs,
reciting the verse of the early moderns, surrounded by the
entwined limbs of lovers, his tie loosened, his body bright in bliss.

Pied Piper on Holiday

After disembarking from the taxi, he locates the room advertised,
the words "discreet" and "private" the only clues given (or needed).
He scans the view of the courtyard, the one less cherished than that of
the village or the mountains: the fruit trees, the mosaics,
the fountain *gurgling*. Was that the word he wanted? He is pleased by
the iron bed with its rough blanket, the paint flaking off the walls,
the porcelain water pitcher and bowl, and the flowered border of
the white cloth crossing the night stand
that serves as the lone ornamentation in the room.

He is familiar with rooms such as this one, and, in fact, prefers them to his
own, with their studied refinement and curios briefly registered: Zagreb,
September 19--, Jarbah Island, ? Such is his manner at home: cautious
but eclectic. It is enough that he does such work by day, well not exactly,
since he often works into the night. Let us say it is enough that this is
his livelihood, to which he is devoted and well-regarded by the few who
know and care. At home, he permits himself some slack, or freedom,
shall we say further. And yet some continuity must be maintained.
He is amused by these pleasures, minor they may be.

He hears voices in reflection, not muffled exactly, but modulated,
and is glad for them, for the tautness of their contribution to
his time here. He remembers the anticipation of long ago, the sounds of
children entering the schoolyard. How he pooled his calm prior to
each lesson, how he drew the children in with his tales, savored the
transformation of their restlessness into rapture. What others would later
call seduction. When he considers the verb "to sack," he thinks
of sackcloth and how, yes, there is a kind of mourning that happens,
or ought to, in any case.

Not only for those children, whose names he whispers: P, M ... . But for others like them who ... . For the children of the children who might have reminded him of their parents. For the chalk dust, for the giggles, for the penmanship shedding tentativeness. Instead, he will catalog objects, to ensure their importance in the history of loveliness. He will hope that the children who might have been will come upon them. And he will remain glad for rooms such as this one, with their blankness, in these varied cities, where certain kinds of connections can be made, where certain kinds of comfort can be found.

Grace Note, in White and Gold

As the candystriper fluffed his pillows,
strands of her black hair agitated the hermetic whiteness.

As the matron scooped up dribbles of gruel,
her hand's trembling created an abstract stain design on his gown.

As the nurse removed his bedpan,
her face clenched with the effort of holding revulsion at bay.

As he crossed the cobbled streets of the mustard-gold hamlet,
noting the vines entwined, murmuring on a balcony's balustrade,

reflecting on the new direction of his thesis,
the light of lines wondrously uncovered, not in the archives,

but in notebooks offered by a crone on a piazza bench,
a gift bequeathed by gnarled hands outside the magistrate's office

how he shivered from gladness and could not release her grip,
as she pooh-poohed and cackled her delight and

how he revisited those vines, their tiny white flowers twinkling above and
to the man tending them, calling to him of their whimsy and resilience,

so that words drifted between petals through fingers skimming iron
so that he couldn't distinguish between lyric, bloom, and baritone gaze

and made his way to the rented chamber and basked on his monk's bed,
fervent to return to the typewriter and the alleys in the day ahead

as he trembled on these white sheets, so different from those never forgotten, in anticipation of the inevitable, the passage to night ongoing,

even then he never relinquished his dream of the elixir of communion, he, so long the debonair recluse, the solitary romantic.

Even on his deathbed he awaited his beloved.

Questions in a Jewish Cemetery

He, who lived for words, did not leave a note.
No e-mail, no voice mail, no text.
Not a single scrap.
Nothing. *Gornisht*. *Efes*.
At least nothing that I could find.
Were you able to find anything?
Now, only the quiet about which he so often wrote.
This ultimate quiet.

If only there was a purpose, as with Szmul Zygielbojm,
the phantom of his dawns,
whom he came to admire, however belatedly.
Was the monster always there,
black lace woven through pink bubblegum chitchat.
Perhaps it hovered ever above.
Or did it arrive stealthily, the panther past twilight.
I'm flailing in this deluge of metaphor. Give us a hand here.

Should we have seen it coming?
How shall we interpret what was apparent,
that which we thought we knew.
How shall we read against re-reading?
Was there a final catalyst?
I won't say "straw."
How could someone who fought for so many years,
for whom exhaustion was never an option, tire finally?

Regina thought he was doing better, perhaps even flourishing.
She said all of that was behind him. By "that," I mean the mother ill so
long, gone so young, the father entombed in tomes, the men who turned
away, the ever shifting entrances to the nation. She insisted so.
She would know if anyone would. There was the reading in June and
an exhibition when was it ... Wasn't there?
Or am I mistaken? I'm sorry I missed them.
How could I possibly have missed both? Where is Regina today?

He was so f***in' tiny.
I wonder how long it took.
Is it wrong to ask?
In death, as in life, he will exist in the margins.
Couldn't the rabbis have bent the rules this once?
Who are these rabbis anyhow?
Surely he repented in the last moments before oblivion.
But then repentance was never his thing, was it.

This corner plot is not so terrible.
The traffic isn't too loud. So much for "quiet."
Should we call this the "my way or the highway" special?
We could plant flowers. He loved irises and tiger lilies and jonquils.
Also something more substantial. Crepe myrtle would work.
The longevity of their flowering found favor in his eyes. And the
talons of the branches, gnarled below, offering their gift to the angels.
Then too how they are neither tree nor bush, but something in between.

Whence his soul? How will it rest?
Where will it alight? Surely not here.
Are these words even permitted?
Is this a eulogy of sorts?
El male raḥamim/God full of mercy …
Adonai ro'i lo eḥsar/The Lord is my shepherd, I shall not want.
Neither seem right here.
I don't know what passages to recite. Do you?

Well, we should be going. Isn't a storm coming?
We could go to his favorite café …
and order the coffee ice cream drink
that the waiter always knew to bring him.
We'll have to deal with the inevitable, you know.
Not to be vulgar.
Not that I care if I am.
Do you?

He wouldn't have cared. You take the art pottery, the books,
the vintage tie collection, the gray linen shirt,
worn just that once by Dmitri on his first opening night.
Still carrying his scent. He asked Dmitri for it and never had it cleaned.
Memento 'Mitri.
You called Dmitri, didn't you?
I'll take the manuscripts,
the music.

לאָיִן *נשמתו*? ווי וועט זי זיך אָפרועןְ?
ווּ וועט זי זיך אָפשטעלן? זיכער נישט דאָ.
צי מעג מען אַפילו אויסרעדן די ווערטער?
איז דאָס אַ מין הספד?
אל מלא *רחמים*/גאָט פֿול מיט רחמים ...
א*דני* רועי לא *אחסר*/גאָט איז מײַן פאַסטעך מיר וועט נישט פֿעלן.
ניין, ביידע טויגן נישט דאָ.
איך ווייס נישט וועלכע פסוקים צו זאָגן. און דו?

נו, לאָמיר גיין. באַלד קומט אַ שטורעם, אַיאָ?
מיר קענען עפעס איבערכאַפן אין זײַן באַליבסטן קאַפֿע ...
און באַשטעלן דאָס קאָװע-אײַזקרעם-געטראַנק
װאָס דער סאַרװער האָט אַלע מאָל געװוּסט אים צו דערלאַנגען.
מיר װעלן דאַרפֿן עפעס אויסאַרבעטן, דו װייסט דאָך.
כ׳װיל נישט זײַן װולגאַר.
כאָטש טאָמער בין איך מאַכט מיר נישט אויס.
און דיר מאַכט יאָ אויס?

אים װאָלט עס נישט געאַרט. נעם דו די קונסט-טעפ, די ביכער,
די אַנטיקע שניפסזאַמלונג, דאָס גרויע ליבװוּנטענע העמד
װאָס דמיטרי האָט דאָס אײן מאָל געטראָגן אויף זײַן ערשטער פֿרעמיערע.
ס׳טראָגט נאָך אַלץ זײַן ריח. ער האָט אים געבעטן בײַ דמיטרין און האָט אים מאָל קײן
נישט געװאָשן.
מעמענטו 'מיטרי.
דו האָסט דמיטרין געלאָזט װיסן, נײן?
איך װעל נעמען די כתב-ידן,
די מוזיק.

רעגינא האט גערמיינט אז ס'איז אים געוואָרן בעסער, קען זײַן אפילו א סך בעסער. זי האט געזאגט אז דאס אלץ איז געווען פֿריִער. ווען איך זאָג "דאָס אַלץ" מיין איך די מאַמע אזוי לאַנג געקרענקט, אַוועק אזוי יונג, דער טאַטע באַגראָבן אין ספרים, די מענער וואָס האָבן זיך אַוועקגעדרייט, די אַרבעטגעבער צום פֿאַלק וואָס בײַט זיך אזוי אָפֿט. אזוי האט זי זיך אײַנגעשפּאַרט. ווען עמעצער וואָלט געוווּסט וואָלט זי דאָס געווען. ס'איז געווען אַ פֿאַרלײענונג אין יוני און אַן אויסשטעלונג ווען איז עס געווען ... ס'איז טאַקע געווען, יאָ? אָדער האָב איך אַ טעות? אַנטשולדיקט מיר וואָס איך האָב זיי פֿאַרפֿעלט. ווי אזוי האָב איך געקעטעט ביידע פֿאַרפֿעלן? ווּ איז הײַנט רעגינא?

ער איז געווען שרעקלעך קליין.
ווי לאַנג האָט געגרמען?
אפשר פֿאַסט נישט צו פֿרעגן?
אין טויט ווי אין לעבן וועט ער לעבן אויף די ראָנדן.
די רבנים האָבן קיין היתר נישט געקענט געפֿינען דאָס איין און אײנציקע מאָל?
נו, און ווער זײַנען זיי אט די רבנים?
זיכער האָט ער תשובה געטאָן האָרן פֿאַרן נישט ווערן.
אָבער צו תשובה איז ער קיין מאָל, צום באַדויערן, נישט געווען פעיִק.

דאָס שטיקל קרקע דאָ בײַם עק איז נישט אַזוי שלעכט.
ס'איז נישטאָ צו פֿיל רעש פֿונעם טראַפֿיק. נו, עס רעדט זיך אַזוי שטיל.
זאָלן מיר דאָס אָנרופֿן די "שאַסײַ-מציאה"?
מיר קענען בלומען פֿלאַנצן. איריסן און טיגער ליליעס און דזשאַנקילן האט ער ליב געהאַט.
אויך עפעס מער ממשותדיק. אפשר קרעפמירטל.
די לאַנגע בליציט זייערע האָט נושא-חן געווען בײַ אים. און די צווײַגן געוואָרן קרעלן, צעקנײלט אונטן, וואָס דערלאַנגן די מתנה צו די מלאכים.
אויך אז זיי זײַנען צו בוים ני קוסט, נאָר עפעס אין צווישן.

קשיות אויף אַ ייִדישן בית-עולם

ער, וואָס האָט געלעבט פֿאַר ווערטער, האָט קיין צעטל נישט איבערגעלאָזט.
נישט קיין בליצבריוו, נישט קיין קול-פֿאַסט, נישט קיין טעקסטאָנזאָג.
נישט קיין שום בּרעקל.
גאָרנישט. נאַדאַ. ריען.
דאָס הייסט, איך האָב גאָרנישט נישט געפֿונען.
האָסטו עפּעס געקענט געפֿינען?
איצט נאָר די שטילקייט וואָס וועגן איר ער האָט אַזוי אָפֿט געשריבן.
די סאַמע שטילקייט.

הלוואַי וואָלט געווען אַ צוועק, אַזוי ווי בײַ שמואל זיגלבוימען,
דער פֿאַנטאָם פֿון זײַנע פֿאַרטאָגן,
וועמען ער איז געקומען באַוווּנדערן, כאָטש שפּעט.
צי איז דאָס פֿאַרזעעניש אַלע מאָל דאָרטן געווען,
שוואַרצע שפּיצן דורכגעוועבט ראָזעווע בלעזל-גומע-פֿלאַפֿלערײַ.
אפֿשר איז עס געהויערט אויבן.
אָדער איז עס ווי אַ גנבֿ געקומען, דער פֿאַנטאָמער נאָך בין-השמשות.
איך פּרוּוו נישט דערטרונקען ווערן אינעם מבול-מעטאַפֿאָר. העלפֿט מיר אַרויס.

האָבן מיר געזאָלט פֿאַראויסזען וואָס וועט געשען?
ווי אַזוי זאָלן מיר אויסטײַטשן דאָס וואָס איז געווען קלאָר,
דאָס וואָס מיר האָבן געמיינט אַז מיר ווייסן שוין.
ווי אַזוי זאָלן מיר לייענען קעגן ווידערלייענען?
צי איז דאָ געווען אַ לעצטע סיבה?
דער "לעצטע שטרוי" טויגט נישט אויף ייִדיש סײַ ווי.
ווי אַזוי איז עמעצער וואָס האָט יאָרן לאַנג זיך געראַנגלט,
פֿאַר וועמען דאָס אויסשעפּן זיך איז קיין מאָל נישט געווען קיין ברירה,
געוואָרן, צום סוף, אויסגעשעפּט?

Regina's Requiem for a Friend

You should have been there.
The blaze from the heavens onto the river
through the floor-to-ceiling windows truly was a flood.
Waterlight, no, *waterfire*. Only FEMA was not needed.
It was possible to perceive shifts in time,
the transition of day to dusk, then, finally, night itself luminous.
You could have observed (if only) that. Had you so elected, that is.
No one would have minded.

You should have been there.
Everyone was there, and yet it was never too much.
I knew this upon entry. I navigated the repartee and the
winding lanes of bodies, searching for you. My hair was held back
with Nana's rhinestone combs that you so admired.
I wore a wine-colored silk number that we found in the vintage
boutique in Louisville. You would have been pleased. I was excited
to see your ensemble. I was sure you were going to outdo yourself.

You should have been there.
I asked about you, but nothing was known. Raphael said you
were coming. He was eager to hear what you would be reading for us.
Lucia performed a cycle of songs from the Spanish Civil War.
Ian and Dusty read from their new two-man show. They open next week!
Jim's new boyfriend, whose name escapes me, rendered an homage to
Nijinsky. Both macho and tender. It was all so very sublime.
You would not have chided me on my hyperbole.

You should have been there.
I kept spotting your type throughout.
Some did not even seem paired.
You would have enjoyed sampling the eye candy;
there was even some petting in the corners. But quite relaxed.
Raphael really went all out with the spread too.
His cooking has garnered raves from the most finicky of palates. And all this from the queen of late-night take-out. Who would have guessed?

You should have been there.
We could have sang the Laverne and Shirley theme song skipping home on the icy flagstones, past the locked park. You could have slept in my bed like old times. Liam is out of town.
We could have had scones with preserves in the morning.
How could you not have been there?
How could I not have insisted? I should have dragged you there.
If you had only been there, you might yet be here.

דו האָסט געזאָלט דאָרטן זײַן.
כ'האָב געזען דײַן טיף אומעטום.
אַ טייל האָבן אַפֿילו נישט אויסגעזען ווי זיי זײַנען אין פֿאַרלעך.
דו וואָלטסט הנאה געהאַט פֿאַרזוכן דעם אויגן-זיסוואַרג;
מע האָט זיך אַפֿילו געליובקעט אין די ווינקלען. אָבער גאָר אָפּגעשפּאַנט.
רפֿאל איז געוועזן אַ בריה מיטן עסן.
זײַן קאָכן האָבן אַפֿילו די גרעסטע פֿינשמעקערס שטאַרק געלויבט. און דאָס אַלץ
פֿון דער מלכּה פֿון שפּעט-נאַכטיקן רעסטאָראַן אַרויסגענעמען. ווער וואָלט געוווסט?

דו האָסט געזאָלט דאָרטן זײַן.
מיר וואָלטן געקענט זינגען דאָס "לאָווערן און שירלי" ליד אַהיימשפּרינגען
אויף די אײַזיקע טראָטואַרן, פֿאַרבײַגייענדיק דעם געשלאָסענעם פּאַרק. דו האָסט געקענט
שלאָפֿן אין בעט ווי אַ מאָל. ליאַם איז איצט נישט אין שטאַט.
מיר האָבן געקענט עסן געבעקס מיט אײַנגעמאַכטס אין דער פֿרי.
ווי אַזוי האָסטו נישט געקענט דאָרטן זײַן?
ווי אַזוי האָב איך זיך נישט געקענט אײַנשפּאַרן? איך האָב דיך געזאָלט אַהינשלעפּן.
ווען דו וואָלטסט נאָר דאָרטן געהאַט געווען וואָלטסטו אפֿשר נאָך אַלץ דאָ געווען.

רעגינאס רעקוויעם צו א פֿרײַנד

דו האָסט געזאָלט דאָרטן זײַן.
דאָס פֿלאַקערן פֿון די הימלען אויפֿן טײַך
דורך די דיל-ביז-סטעליע-פֿענצטער איז טאַקע געווען אַ מבול.
וואַסערליכט, נײן, וואַסערפֿײַער. נאָר "פֿימאַ" האָט מען נישט געדאַרפֿט.
עס איז געווען מיגלעך צו דערזען ענדערונגען אין צײַט,
דעם איבערגאַנג פֿון טאָג אין בין-השמשות אַרײַן, און צום סוף, נאַכט אַליין ליכטיק.
דו וואָלסט געקענט (נאָר) דאָס זען. דאָס הייסט, ווען דו וואָלסט אַזוי באַשלאָסן.
ס'וואָלט קיינעם נישט געאַרט.

דו האָסט געזאָלט דאָרטן זײַן.
יעדער איז געווען דאָרטן, און דאָך איז עס קיין מאָל נישט געווען צו פֿיל.
כ'האָב דאָס געוווּסט ווען איך בין אַרײַן. זוכנדיק דיר האָב איך נאָוויגירט דאָס
געפֿלאַפֿל און די געשלענגטע סטעזשקעס גופֿים. די האָר זײַנען פֿאַרבונדן
מיט דער באָבעס רײַנשטײן-קעמלעך וואָס דו האָסט אַזוי ליב געהאַט.
כ'האָב געטראָגן אַ ווײַן-קאָלירט זײַדן קלייד וואָס מיר האָבן געפֿונען אינעם אַנטיקקראָם
אין לויוויל. דו וואָלסט געווען צופֿרידן. כ'האָב זייער געוואָלט
זען דײַן גאַרניטער. זיכער אַז דו וועסט זיך אַליין אַריבערשטײַגן.

דו האָסט געזאָלט דאָרטן זײַן.
כ'האָב זיך נאָכגעפֿרעגט נאָך דיר, אָבער קיינער האָט גאָרנישט נישט געהאַט געהערט.
רפֿאל האָט געזאָגט אַז דו וועסט קומען. ער איז געווען נײַגעריק צו הערן וואָס דו וועסט
פֿאַר אונדז פֿאָרלייענען.
לוטשיאַ האָט געזונגען אַ ציקל לידער פֿונעם שפּאַנישן בירגערקריג.
איאַן און דאַסטי האָבן פֿאַרגעלייענט פֿון זייערע נײַער פֿיעסע פֿאַר צוויי אַקטיאָרן.
די פֿיעסע וועט זיך עפֿענען די קומעדיקע וואָך!
דזשימס נײַער געליבטער כ'האָב שוין פֿאַרגעסן ווי ער הייסט האָט אָפּגעגעבן כּבֿוד
ניזשינסקין. סײַ מאַטשו סײַ מילד. ס'איז אַלץ געווען גאָר געהויבן.
דו וואָלסט מיך נישט אויסגעמוסרט צוליב מײַן גוזמא.

Crossing the Big Box Store Parking Lot

Bloomington, Indiana, 2010

Once we had these things:
matter drawn from the Lord's Earth transformed then sent to
brick buildings with vast floors and windows
from which products, essential or otherwise,
shaped by hands, our hands, emerged.

Once we had these things:
resolve to insist on safety and dignity,
savvy to galvanize our peers, to make our muscle feared,
to refuse the dread instilled by the scabs and the Pinkertons
and their employers, pronouncing our fate in a haze of cigar smoke.

Once we had these things:
a main street with shops individually owned,
signs hand-painted in curlicue, swaying in the breeze,
with restaurants whose meals were constructed plainly, with gusto:
today, tuna casserole; tomorrow, beef stew.

Once we had these things:
a home with three bedrooms, a swatch of green for Maura's white roses,
a breakfront to store Nana's china, unchipped after all these years,
a fund to transport our children beyond the baseline,
to advance beyond ourselves, to revise their corner of the cosmos.

Once we had these things:
an ability to live past 1.5 paychecks,
a belief in the power of our toil to effect lasting good,
the certainty that we would not languish, shivering, over grates,
beseeching, with our smallest ones, indifferent passersby for a quarter.

Now we rush to the behemoths for the bargains
spun and welded and woven and sold by hands, "other" hands,
bereft of the protections for which we struggled and won.
Campaign flyers flutter by boarded windows where once we labored.
Our towns drift into tumbleweed, as if en route to Nineveh or Persepolis.

Now every Labor Day, after the parade and barbecue, both diminished,
her teeth rotting, her stoop sparkling, her rocking chair squeaking,
the drumbeats and burgers echoing through the cricketsong,
Mabel, who never misses much, somehow sees this:
her niece Caitlin placing white roses on Maura's tombstone.

Temporary Outcasts

Here there can be no question of panhandling.
Can I bum a cigarette?
is posed a tad below irony,
delivered with directness,
lubricated by a twinkle,
belying the panic bubbling through studied off-handedness.
Refusal is not expected nor is it an option.
If ever I am in your shoes ...
If ever I hunger thus, let a kind stranger ...
In this realm, needs are met.

Once a major percentage of the folk,
then sprinkled widely among them,
they now congregate ubiquitously,
in front of workplaces or taverns or transit stations,
if increasingly farther from the entrance.
In often the most inclement of conditions—
hail, hurricane, as if pink slips were imminent—
they can be seen and overheard in clusters, inhaling,
swapping jokes or recipes or scores or stories,
hair and ties and scarves flapping in the gale.

Even with the unambiguity of the research,
even with the bravura of the whistleblowers,
even as the ad campaigns become more inventive,
even as the warnings grow more dire and the tsk-tsk-s ever louder,
even as Menasheh visits his middle-aged aunt hacking in the hospice,
cravings are fed, not in cells or cellars or alleys,
but emblazoned at the peripheries of open view.
Community is configured and cannot quite be dispersed,
not unlike the wraiths rising from toxic root
that seem to vanish elegantly into November mist.

Black and White (and Green) and Red All Over

In the moment before a paper cut draws blood, anything can happen.
Fate itself is suddenly open-ended, free of borders.
How paper ought to be held—edges away from fingertips—
is suddenly foregrounded. Too late.

Corners—sites of convergence, spying, or shelter—now rever-
berate with echoes of childhood punishment. Habit is cursed, so too
        carelessness.
Once a neutral canvas to be utilized for any cause at all,
to be something useful for other than itself, paper is suddenly

a source of danger. Infection is not unlikely. The words, in this case
a memorandum about network service shutdown, are humdrum.
The paperless society has not materialized. Identity thieves comb the
trash so readily available; you are still summoned by post for jury duty.

The shredder truck can be seen discreetly inching out of the garage.
Evoking goose feathers, white shards overflow its belly.
The master hackers chuckle in the cobalt glow of their screens. To
realize their menace they need not leave their lairs.

Severed from the earth's magnetic fields, you stumble
over pavement and cobblestone alike. Only with gadgets can your
breath approach coherence. And yet you remember the frayed silk
sleeve of your robe when you read that text message,

how you wished it was a note handwritten on textured paper,
propped against a lacquered vase on a rococo writing table.
Yes, blood appears. A droplet moving into torrent. Even as you force
yourself to grope for inevitability, its destination eludes you.

The stones cannot provide protection, that's clear. The tree trunks will
be hacked, pulp into slate for the environmental manifesto.
The encircling devoted are scorned as "hippies" and "huggers."
Careful, you there on the sidelines, hiding, hovering.

The trees and their wardens will exact revenge.
Nothing radical at this point, to be sure,
but with insistence, portents of the apocalypse,
natural and psychic, to come.

Breakfast in the Basement (with Bureaucrats)

For Greg Marcangelo

Here we huddle against the silhouettes of trees
slicing whitely into the almost-royal blue wall
that evoke somehow the scene in Tarkovsky's debut
of Masha and the soldier in the forest the light the cold
and Masha's hunger and terror and courage the kiss above the trench
that cannot be lost in the gunfire and muck
for the young Master willed it just so and so it shall ever be

Here we huddle in the basement without window
the only light the fluorescent one humming above
to break first bread before the day of processing
and assembling and piecing and foraging order from chaos
guardians of treasure as they assure us but only to skim creativity
to take stock and categorize forbidden to linger
for this is not a mid-summer porch by a lake in the mountains
and there is no iced raspberry lemonade in hand

Here we revel in the latest words and images of the weekly
still in print after these many years
one of the few surviving bastions of wit and panache and
commitment to investigation and reflection
an oasis in the din of demagoguery that you and I dissect at length
for we marvel at the extent of its reach at the regularity of its release
at the precariousness of our victories of long ago

And just as the word flair and ads for subdued sparkles can't efface
its combativeness so here we are insisting over scrambled
eggs and gruel on the marriage of elegance and liberation on good and
glamour before rising to face our backlogs grateful that the taxpayers
still sustain this work we love and so here we are dreaming of gems
unearthed that will flay the creep of tedium as Masha envelopes us
in her enigmatic embrace as the weapons of war are arrayed just so
by the bureaucrats there they are across the river

Bacchanal at Empire's End

Gone was the day when they could frolic, bejeweled,
in palaces and playgrounds for a few to see
(and more to peek at).
Even stone walls crowned with barbed wire could be scaled.
There was simply too much at stake.
Instead, the oligarchs decided to congregate
in unmarked cavernous expanses.
Discretion was now essential.

Vases from (foolishly) forgotten dynasties were installed
in niches crafted from centuries of water dripping on rock.
Carpets and cushions, divans and hassocks
were strewn artfully about.
Caviar and truffles and other delicacies appeared without summons.
Wines of the rarest vintage, flowed freely, as if from bottomless cellars.
Castrati, with their eagerness and practiced jollity,
were called upon to entertain.

Young women and young men,
their buttocks glimmering in the gloom,
were utilized for entertainment of other sorts.
The word "perversion" was bandied about as if itself a witticism,
toppling the ladies, with their heaving décolletage,
into fits of fuschia laughter. Now that they were here,
they could not believe they had not tried these positions before.
Truly something for everyone, they reflected.

There was whispering of discontent, to be sure.
Occasionally stories of suffering of the most grisly sort,
both on the war fronts and closer to home, intruded.
But there were methods of dealing with provocateurs, who in any case,
had only themselves to blame. A nod here, a word there. Problem solved.
Our right to the pursuit of happiness shall not be denied,
the oligarchs insisted, fingering the cracks of anxiety
just dawning in the sanctum of their subterranean revelry.

The People of the Book ... Without Books?

The wives whispered at the butcher and in the market
and on departing the bathhouse after ritual immersion;
the husbands in the house of study
and while selecting the citrons and palm branches.
They shook their heads and clicked their tongues,
looking down so as not to see.

It was shocking, as you can imagine, and yet not
in that way that only decrees affecting the People of the Book can be.
Only just released, it was already plastered on bulletin boards
outside prayer halls and on doors and telephone poles.
Seemingly ubiquitous. Yet no one quite knew how they had gotten there
since no one had been seen posting them. *Is there a traitor among us?*

A meeting in the synagogue was convened on Tuesday evening.
After long prayers composed for occasions such as this,
shouting erupted. The rabbi proved unable to control the frenzy,
which could well have been heightened by the days of fasting.
The burly beadle and his henchmen, whose physical prowess
was feared by Jew and gentile alike, had to restore order.

Even if temptations of the flesh could be completely filtered out
to save us and our children from ruin,
the synagogue's chief benefactor wondered,
and that is far from a given for cunning is the Evil Inclination,
could legal permission actually be granted?
How shall we pray on the Sabbath and on holidays
when electronic devices are forbidden?

And how dare we depart from the path of our ancestors,
they who touched and swayed over and died for these holy books
and from the ground below where the fragments are buried,
cried the cantor in intonation normally reserved for the Days of Awe.
And how shall the weekly Torah portion be recited,
the words that unite our people in homeland and diaspora,

for surely scrolls will not be spared, wept the Torah reader,
so young and already renowned across several provinces
for a style of cantillation stunning in its
precision of enunciation and mastery of melody. We shall descend
underground. No, we shall study the ways of the martyrs.
Enough! God will reveal the means, the rabbi said, resuming prayer.

Leaves rustling in gratitude, only the trees rejoiced.

Bystanders

The shades of the alerts had multiplied.
Now chartreuse, rust, and silver were to be heeded.
These differences had to be mastered if peril were to be eluded.
We consulted the pamphlets obtained at subway kiosks,
frantically trying to memorize their meanings.
However, the emphatic tones of the commands
only underscored their essential vagueness:
Always be on the lookout for ... Be aware of your surroundings ...
Be sure not to ... Be suspicious ...
When a passenger next to us coughed, we envisioned lethality
clotting our lungs and fled into the next car.

The streets were no more reassuring.
Flyers in oversized fonts and fluorescent colors had been wheatpasted
everywhere. They warned of coming scourges, spectacular in scope
and focused in debilitation, and offered remedies of various kinds.
Rare plants grown deep within tropical jungles, or what was left of them,
had been imported and could now be obtained by contacting
so-and-so who lived just a few blocks from the Capitol. Looking around,
we jotted down the numbers. Was it more dangerous to go or to stay
away, we wondered. The blogs and listservs tucked away in
corners of the virtual universe blared predictions yet more dire.
We avoided those altogether. We had to set limits, after all.

Entering and exiting the city-state had become a gargantuan undertaking.
Gone were the days of removing shoes and belts and metal.
Strip searches, body cavities included, were now mandated.
The elderly, the very young, the pregnant were not exempted.
Many did, in fact, try for exemptions. Influence had never been a more
precious commodity. To no avail. Everyone was mortified by the sight
of a venerable peace activist who had stood down the tanks and guns
of heavily armed soldiers reduced to bawling as his buttocks were parted
and probed by the guards. We turned our backs in solidarity.

There was little else we could do. Besides, we were next.
We knew what would happen if we tried anything.

We now rarely ventured forth from our resident cells.
We had no illusions about their superior safety. The authorities had long ago seen to that. Only we had to rest more. It was not simply a question of our state of mind. Our bodies themselves had changed. From all the scanning and sneezing and poking and prying, innards had blanched and constricted. For all the talk of antibodies, we had weakened considerably.
We knew we had to keep at it, as our leaders commanded.
To flail or fail now was not an option, they insisted. And what would happen to our children if we faltered, we fretted dully.
At bedtime, we caressed their faces in desperation, reading to them from legends and fairy tales we had once thought terrifying.

Empty Nesters

The plums plummeted early on Bunker Hill Road this year,
toppled by a misalignment of climactic signals
or a rare eagerness convened by the envoys of spring.
No one was quite sure.

Their skins were rent by the fall
or rather its aftermath.
Some had sought safety and were, in fact, gingerly avoided;
most were squashed in the stampede of commuters,
the stamp of stiletto heels visible upon inspection.

The pavement beneath was transformed into a kaleidoscope
of bruise and mortification.
The color of the ruin resembled that of the trees' leaves,
offspring mirroring parent.

Indeed, some of the branches had become ragged, leaves sparse,
barely budding—a line of treasured, if flawed, canopy shade.
Equally unexpectedly, armed with manuals and shears and
synchronicity, guerilla landscapers descended one morning to clip
the branches of the plum trees. Their resolve was noted with unease.

Perhaps they aim to revive the blood; perhaps they seek to console.
Perhaps they wish to ease the agony of the parents
over this indifference to their children,
crushed before their time.

At Rachel's Tomb

*...Rachel weeps for her children; she refuses to be consoled
on her children, for they are no more* —Jeremiah 31:14

At first he thought they must be in the wrong place.
Instead of the domed sand-colored structure on a
grassy knoll pictured in the needlepoint
over which Mother had labored for so long and
which hung in the hallway while she yet lived
and now hangs on his brother's living room wall,
there was only a gray concrete box and a parking lot
fronted by a locked yellow gate. So this was it?

Entry on foot was forbidden.
On that the soldier would not budge,
despite Margalit's entreaties in her flirtatious Holy Tongue.
They pleaded with one driver, who would only take Margalit,
because she could not allow a male stranger into her car.
Happily, a scantily clad Italian scholar happened by and waved
them both in, a free spirit sharing the bounty of her wheels.
Their luck was changing!

It took time to adjust to the gloom.
Beggars of both genders greeted them with appeals for alms.
He and Margalit drifted apart without word,
instinctively attuned to the strictures of segregation. When in Rome ...
He soon came upon the prayer and study hall. The *bimah*,[1]
with its maroon velvet cover protected by plastic, centered the room,
the cacophony of men in study, careening all around it.
Then he thought, Rome?!

---

1 — *bimah* (Hebrew; *bimeh* in Yiddish): the platform in the synagogue from which the Torah is read

This could be a *shtibl*[2] in Boro Park or Monroe, New York.
He drifted back out into the corridors, skimming the walls,
hoping to find her, if even just a trace. Above. Below. Anywhere.
Thorough was his search. Where is the Matriarch's
resting place constructed in stitch by Mother as if brick by brick?
Where is the copper tomb that adorned
the green leather clasped prayer book from which
Mother murmured entreaties of her own.

The Matriarch who died in giving birth to her second son;
Mother who lost so many children of her own.
The Matriarch buried en route, hovering in a liminal space;
Mother buried in XX at age ##. Where are they now?
Then, in exiting, he glanced up and there it was: the tomb just as he
remembered—replete with grassy knoll. Only it was rendered on the
compound's wall, a billboard advertising a destination just a few feet
away. Was the mural a hallucination? A postmodern riddle?

As the Italian scholar expanded on Rome and the Jews and the zealots
and her itinerary, as Margalit offered directions to Jerusalem,
he found himself weeping, weeping for lands contested and residents
queuing at checkpoint not far away, weeping for children
smithereened ensconced in shrines of their own,
weeping for prayer books misplaced and prayers shimmering out of reach,
weeping for mothers who never reached the Promised Land,
weeping for mothers lost in childbirth and Mother's losses from childbirth.

By the side of the road to Efrat he joined Rachel in weeping.

---

2 — *shtibl* (Yiddish): small Hasidic house of prayer

The Imminent Arrival of Gleaners

He sometimes thinks of it as a field lying fallow,
as if ensnared in the seventh-year status
mandated in Exodus 23:11:
And in the seventh year
you must let it rest and refrain from it
and the poor of your nation shall eat from it
and the remains shall be consumed by the wild beasts of the field.

Only it's neither field nor fallow.
It's just a weed-laced lot in front of a train station
whose nakedness has rendered it remarkably devoid
of broken beer bottles and candy bar wrappers.
Passersby walk or drive past, mostly quickly, the day ahead or gone,
apparently indifferent to its minimal charms.
Occasionally, the brave or desperate will come to toss a ball or a Frisbee.

Yet for all its homeliness, the lot has garnered outside attention.
Space is precious in the city, the developers insist. There is potential here.
A meeting, with graphs and projected revenues, is hurriedly convened.
In shabby halls dense with anxiety, neighbors scan documents,
skeptical over assurances of increased values.
Our savings have never seemed more shallow, they fret,
our futures never more fragile.

How surprised he was then when the next morning
he found the lot blanketed in flowers.
Perhaps it was a visitation, a fist raised against spreadsheets;
perhaps an installation by Christo and Jeanne-Claude.
He wanted to race unthinkingly between them,
to detect the strands of his breath isolated and magnified,
to be winded by and enveloped in purpleness or lavenderdom.

Only he could not enter the lot turned field.
Suddenly wily,
the flowers deflected his footwork,
unimpressed with his dance and dive
over and under their petals, his flit between their stems.
The seventh year has not passed, the flowers murmured,
the poor and later the feral dogs shall be here soon to dine.

II. In the Gleaning

To the Formica Gardens

Imagine an expanse of lawn,
or shall we say, meadow,
or perhaps even meadows,
bordered by forest, tranquil and generous.
Flowers, out of bed, unlabeled,
are placed strategically for inspiration.

It is always autumn or spring here,
the climate accommodating, undemanding.
The "barns," intermittently chipped, offer interiors for reflection:
whitewashed walls that resist the clinical; beveled glass windows
that open outward onto the picturesque. A tray of food is placed
outside the door, a twin bed to repel distraction.

And then delete this image.
It is merely borrowed from brochures wavy from dried drool.
Come here instead, here where papers, mostly bills,
some flyers, are strewn, here where books totter,
here where lines are composed above a Formica desk
as evening dawns, culled from an imagined notebook.

See instead stanzas sketched on the avenue or on the stuck
subway train; the stench of sardined summer bodies remembered.
Amidst cussing billowing outward, here is a glimpse of an anonymous
soul in gray at ease, contained. Graffiti drilled through reverie.
A high dive upwards, then a spiral descent for breath.
What time is it anyway?

Panic pangs and day sweats are cast aside.
As the tunnel narrows, as the ticket booths vanish,
rats congregate with dreams beneath the fluorescent drone
to the melodic accompaniment of an unidentified physical plant.
Here, have some quarter-moon prickly pears.
Welcome to my artists' colony.

Yermiyahu the Book Peddler

It could be a day cloudless, geometric to the touch.
It could be a day metallic, heavens dully closing in.
It does not matter.
The question of portent is of no relevance here.
You will see a figure pulling a wagon
stooped over the horizon.
First a dot and then coming into focus.
And the calls that grow louder:
"*Poetry! Poetry for sale! Poetry! Poetry for sale!*"

The housewives swing open their windows;
their bosoms dangle listlessly.
The children gather around the figure, his hat askew,
poking under the volumes,
rifling through his pockets for coins or lollipops.
When none materialize, a few tug at his pants.
One even kicks his shins,
if with little enthusiasm.
No rocks are thrown. At least that.

A dandy scans the jumble.
Something for my sweetie, he says,
dark locks veiling the skepticism beginning to coalesce.
Away he saunters, off to the flower vendor, no doubt.
(Or perhaps to the confectionary, where he will send the girls in pink
into peals of giggles with his impersonation of the book peddler.)
Mina, the mayor's maiden aunt,
fingers the amulet tucked beneath her collar,
leafs to locate the lines that can encapsulate
the enormity of her inchoate desire.

It could be a night starless.
It could be a night ravaged by lightning.
It does not matter.
The question of tangibility is of no relevance here.
You will see a figure just below the horizon,
static in size and proportion,
skirts billowing about, crumpled on a silk blanket,
and a kerosene lamp swaying above the wagon.
You will hear the calls now murmured,
careening through the concerto of night birds:
"*Poetry! Poetry for sale! Poetry! Poetry for sale!*"

Semi-Somnia

I am a student of night.
Without sun or even moon I flower.
Well, not really. Instead, I clumsily cobble together
a crazy quilt of slumber and sentrydom.

The meteorites, braced for displacement,
prove ideal for scooping up my tears, my principal nocturnal emissions.
The south star, in its generosity, leads my ever-more humbled frame/
expands my narrowed terrain into a grove stretching into infinite.

There, equations in mind, compass in hand,
I decipher gradations, the ebbing of onyx into sapphire into lapis
then suddenly cornflower. Fur and leaf rustle into shelter's bustle;
bird and baboon and baby call and respond.

I register changes in tenor and tone—
the chirps, the cheeps, the caws, the *glups*—
in the spreadsheets of my fingertips,
trying to deflect them from the quicksand around my feet.

I hear slumber lumbering finally towards dawn,
as I wonder how *dormir* can possibly connect to dormant.
I glance down to glimpse
that my needle can't stop breakdancing,

that my fingers are slipping on the wet well walls,
that my bloom is now adroop in the fade from black,
that I am abraded by the braiding of whisper and whimper and
remnants of weeping, the terror of relinquishing darkness.

Mirage

Where would I be without my baggage,
those soiled, well-fondled playthings.
Would I glide through airport security
as others pummel their fists in fury, in vain
against my plexiglass fullbody condom.
Would the concierge and the porter,
having settled me in my chamber,
pore over the *pensione* in search of my things
only to smile in relief then shock at their absence.
Would I saunter or would I skip
down the boulevards and lanes of foreign capitals,
without map or camera
or parasol or *parapluie* or even sunblock,
turning heads with my sprite and joie-de-vivre.
Would the City of Light adjust its glow for too bright was mine.

Who would I be without my baggage,
those markers that have rendered me into me.
Would my height dazzle necks to crane in wonder:
Look how close to the origins of rain!
Would my skin, so smooth without salve,
beckon to touch.
Would my curls sparkle as if express from nature
the better to shield the delight restrained in my eyes.
Who would I be if other yarns were spun,
if other legends were imbibed,
if other books were given to read,
if the same books were read otherly,
if other rulings on other desires were inscribed.
Who would I be if I were other than this:
a little boy crouching in bramble and dusk,
looking over his shoulder,
gathering star dust from the gods.

Cataclysm in Hebrew Class, or,
How Yermiyahu First Went Astray

Yeladim yi-yeladot/ boys and girls today is a special day
you have learned many songs you have danced in a circle
you have performed Friday night in Friday morning class
you have drawn pictures of ritual objects such as the menorah and the
shofar who can tell me what the *shofar* is and when is it blown a ram's
horn and on Rosh ha-Shanah *metsuyan*/excellent Yael
you have sampled many tasty treats such as *ḥalah* and *'ugiyot*/cookies
Nahum what is your favorite *'ugiyah*
ah chocolate chip *ṭa'im me'od*/very tasty
no we cannot have *'ugiyot* today Gavriel
perhaps next Friday *aval ha-yom*/but today is the day
when you will begin writing the *alef bet*/the Hebrew alphabet this is one
of the most important days in your life remember each letter is sacred
for this is the Holy Language and the sages
our wise men say *otiyot makhkimot*/letters enlighten
make you smart each letter will give you a key to the words of our people
I am going to pass out a *maḥberet*/powder blue notebook
to each and every one of you so that you can practice your cursive hand
your handwriting and I want you to take care of it to consider it
mamash/literally as holy as a *sidur*/prayer book and *Ḥumash*/Pentateuch
which you will get one day does everyone now have a *maḥberet*
now this is an *alef* this is your first step Gedalyah how can you possibly
remember your first baby step so study its shape I will draw it again
and now the letter *bet* a little easier huh who can tell me a word that
begins with *bet bubah*/doll begins with the letter *bet*
ṭov me'od/very good Rivkah *bayit*/house also *nakhon*/correct
no baby does not begin with *bet* Yosef baby is an English word
but the sound b-b-b is the same now who wants to come to the *luaḥ*/
the blackboard and write an *alef* Yermiyahu wants to try *ṭov* who can
tell me what Yermiyahu did wrong that is correct Uri the half-circle
of the *alef* has to be written before the line Hebrew always goes from
right to left that is how it is different from languages that use the

A-B-C why does it matter Yermiyahu you ask I will tell you because
that is what separates the Hebrew alphabet from most other alphabets
you must start the *alef* with a half-circle on the right and not with a line on
the left it doesn't matter that in the end it looks the same it must be written
in the correct order this is an important lesson do you understand this is
important for Yermiyahu and the whole class I do not
wish to embarrass Yermiyahu *ḥas ve-ḥalilah*/God forbid don't
cry for it is said that he who embarrasses someone in public loses his
place in the world to come *ṭov yeladim vi-yeladot* that is enough for today
Yermiyahu you may sit down now

Safety Net

I still remember my first trip to the library housed in the attic
of the mansion turned school, browsing the shelves,
boy brimming with first library card, a card with blue lines
tucked into each book, author and title typed, due date stamped,
to be heeded lest privileges be revoked, the joy of speaking with the
librarian, a survivor (for even then we knew the tattoo as signifier)
gifted to us from Germany via Auschwitz, whose graciousness
we treasured even if we couldn't fathom it.

I still remember my first trip to the branch of the public library housed in
a modern brown brick one-story building. Here, possibility danced
before us on walls (and shelves between them) bulging. Here was an
expanse of gleaming white linoleum, here were mats on which to
recline as the librarian read to us in tones sonorous and measured as our
teacher let go. Here were Amelia and Ramona and most gloriously,
Betsy and Tacy (and later Tib), whose antics we came to celebrate.
We didn't yet know to be fidgety.

I still remember my first visit to the yeshiva library housed in a room
across from the bathroom and the lockers. How small and dark it was,
more like a closet (!), devoid of chairs, with only a paucity of materials
having escaped the censors, seemingly constructed to satisfy a state
requirement, so different from the study halls filled with sacred works
in other buildings. Yet even here I managed to extract some comfort
not from any particular text that would give name to the unspeakability
of me, but from the shapes of words, the care in their arrangement.

I wish I could say that I still remember my first visit to my college library or the sort of building that housed it. Here my nostalgia fails me. Perhaps because I had struggled against such opposition to enroll in the citadel of secularism, the library seemed anticlimactic. Perhaps because I knew there would be other nooks to which to escape, such as the student newspaper with its other misfits. Perhaps I never knew if I would get to finish, given the expense and the opprobrium. Better not get too attached, I might well have thought.

I wish I could say there was a path from there to here, that from those trips I found a calling. Perhaps. All that is certain, however, is that which is described above, and too the whispering peculiar to halls lined with books, the light ebbing as closing time nears and selection decisions loom, the rustling and stamping of books at the circulation desk, and the relief, however temporary,
from the taunts and fists and kicks assembled outside the library door.

In the MRI Machine

Crammed into tube skull in vise
musing on the fragility of bone and breath
the ingenious ways that the body can be afflicted
for being on the wrong side displeasing to those in power
only this is for the benefit of humanity
the detection of growth alien perhaps still available for excision
science at its most benign if only its architects could have
executed a tool life-saving that did not so resemble a coffin

and the drilling who knew there was such a range of
distinctly disagreeable sounds a cacophony no a symphony of
terror as if John Cage on crack and John Zorn on Quaaludes
had collaborated at Yaddo and this was the result
once I thought I detected a sound incongruously lighthearted
that resembled Pac-Man and I remembered how my friends and I
would sneak away from yeshiva to play it in the nearby grocery store
was this now my punishment

until the technician in the booth Adam is his name alerted me to the
scan to come four minutes he said and I was so grateful to him for his
kindness for he did not have to do so and I tried to disentangle the
immediate fear of being buried alive from the less immediate one of what
this test would reveal whether I would soon actually wish I was still in
this moment of unknowing a state not of innocence but of before-ness
pre-diagnosis pre-verdict of facing the end before my time even as
I wondered if there is such a thing as at one's time

and so I slipped back to when my head was resting
on Mother's belly as she murmured the Psalms
Al tirḥak mimeni ki tsarah ḳerovah; ki en 'ozer/
Be not distant from me for trouble is near; and there is none to help
as the fan whirred and the needlepoint its holes soon to be filled by
thread so vivid so fine was put momentarily aside so my head was not
in vise but under hands rising and falling with the movement of her
breath and her legs were extended her veins blue but not yet varicose

to a place and time of love complete not dependent on a particular
action or achievement or body in such and such condition
a witness to a communion between God and supplicant
slipping between prayers feeling their touch on mother's translucent
arms the landscape of her body whose nearly every plane and hill
I knew then and know still and as the clatter and clang of
science jangled my every nerve I prayed that I might be
spared her agony that these prayers

might yet be answered even if mine no ours for her (those many years in
and out of rooms worse than the one I'm in now with their whispering and
hope and confusion and stoicism such effort at control the toll it all took)
were not in the end answered even as I knew there was no justice really in
any of this all of it a race having to do with time and fortune and genetics
and access and the right doctor seen at the right moment for he might well
have gone yachting I did so pray into this din take me to her love
not her end let that particular circle not come full

Pleasure Palace, 1988

I fled the Talmud to sojourn
among men in tan trench coats and hats pulled low over brow.
The competing fragrances of Mr. Clean and man sting my eyes
so I grope for a path, stumbling from one booth into another
in search of the salvation, however fleeting, refused by the *Amora'im/*
Talmudic sages and their disciples and descendants.
Love in all the wrong places, my friends would later diagnose.

In cavernous cheeks and glittering eyes
the plague has taken up residence here on this lagoon.
I cannot help but notice this.
Soon I will see it everywhere.
Even with their insistence on cleanliness and purity,
the Jews can't circumvent this plague.
One wrong move and there's no turning back.

Under the flashing red lights of the marquee,
the itinerant preachers on the sidewalks outside
chant their chorus of warning and damnation:
Heed His word! The fires of hell await you!
Outside, others hurry by in a cocoon of indifference,
but inside the preachers' agitation grows more potent, despite the
easy-listening love songs crooning on the p.a. system.

I learn to master the milliseconds of a glance—
when to stay, when to follow, when to search anew.
The fate of a night or a life is determined at breakneck speed
as I seek to avoid breaking my neck on the perpetually wet floors.
Bodies on display, in stasis and in motion,
possibility in every permutation (except the one most sought),
form the backdrop to this portable panorama.

All of this I note as I wait and hope and roam
and take recess from the hunt.
My muscles are cramped, my jaws ache,
my mouth is sore, my eyes are bloodshot.
And yet my skills are not unwelcome.
I have proven to be a nimble apprentice here,
as I never was in the Talmudic zone.

I came of age among men in tan trench coats
and hats pulled low over brow.
I return to their sights and sounds and smells and their touch, even
if I've never left them, to their arcades and cinemas and storefronts
now long shuttered by the mayor the police the chat rooms
the clever phones pleasure made virtual
even as I wonder how future generations will come to discover shame.

Ephemera

The tails of your snores tickle the nipples of the constellations.
Your shaved head gleams against the pillow,
a lone discernible character on a rain-drenched rice paper scroll.
Your massive arms enfold me,
perhaps for protection,
perhaps against flight.
Will I ever know?
My tongue wanders between the tendrils of your pelt,
as I unearth the landmarks of your day—
the spoken word in the bodega,
Dunkin' Donuts hazelnut coffee,
and most prominently,
your habitual South Indian take-out.
Your pistol winks flirtatiously on a distant chair.
I stir,
harden as your grip tightens.
Is kissing permitted? How about a cuddle then?

The stars embark on their retreat,
oblivious to my protestation.
Dawn's menace presses against the curtains.
The phrase "Stay away, Day!" stomps
through my torpor like a right-wing protest chant.
Your fingers trace a path to their favorite vacation spots.
Then you are arisen, a rhapsody of black into blue.
Soon, the running water; later, the foggy glass—
the lanyard of dread, inevitability, and song.
Now suddenly you are alongside,
pulling on the polyester pants that suit you so.
A leather jacket materializes.
Before the slap on my ass,
against the vista of improbably flocked wallpaper,
I consider to ask:
May we visit, some day, even some night,
in a place other than this?

Streaker in Stasis

Was that you I saw
on exiting Balducci's
frowning on my avalanche of delicacies
as if traces of Belgian chocolate smeared my lips
your silhouette skulking between the pipes of scaffolding
surrounding the women's prison turned branch library

Was that you I saw
near the rear of the gallery auditorium
head in hand
as if mortified as if delighted
three seats away from the nudnik who kept haranguing
the experimental filmmaker on the necessity of narrative

Was that you I saw
on line for the exhibition
with its pop and buzz and flash
and the oohs and ahs the stamp of admiration
with your hermeneutic of skepticism in place
the red ink of you etched in your forehead

Was that you I saw
at the rally in Municipal Plaza protesting police brutality
or was it on the avenue collecting signatures
willing pedestrians to stop just short of drowning
in your eyes so green
scrawling their signatures on the petition as if transfixed

Was that you I sensed
while staring out my fleabag digs at the barbed wire
the coital creaking overhead
the drip-drop of the bathroom sink
the fluorescent lamp droning
the cascade of your kisses on the nape of my bruised neck

Travels in Brooklyn After Midnight

"Come on in. I'm Dame Maggie.
My fellas call me the Other Dame Maggie,"
she said, never clarifying the identities of the "fellas."
Hobbling from the massive front door
to the grand gone shabby staircase,
she shook her cane upwards at the first door on the left.
Her elderly sheepdog,
his fronds visible everywhere, tail flopping feverishly,
delighted in the scents of the considerably more elderly
tomes in the boxes we lugged up to Ezra's new digs,
which shocked us with its floral wallpaper
and French provincial reproductions.
How will Socrates and Gramsci breathe in here? Ezra asked,
his auburn locks flattened in perspiration,
his body constricted in chagrin.
They've managed in worse, I offered,
already halfway down the stairs for
more boxes of books.
And so it went:
up and down until near evening's end.

"I'm up late. Don't forget to kiss me good-night," Dame Maggie said
as we ventured out in our exhaustion into the environs of Caribbean
Brooklyn. Sampling the jerk chicken over the single plastic table
in the glare of the 24-hour take-out joint, I offered consolation
over the departure of yet another of his blonde damsels
and well wishes on this new start with the Dame and the fellas,
whoever they may be.
There was so much I wanted to say to Ezra,
about the possibilities for alliance,
the symbiosis even between philosophy and poetry,
the quest for the tangible, the celebration of the ideal,
a marriage of mathematics and meter and music,

and how in fact there could never have been discord between them.
There was so much more too I might have said
on how I could come to his room from my apartment at any time,
sneak away from the none-too-pleased vigilance of my own landlady,
more than a few immigrant neighborhoods away,
even if travel within Brooklyn was limited by the subway's designers,
even if the borders of identity were surely fluid, ever debated, by the
philosophers and poets and psychologists and now the cultural theorists,
to name just a few, if only ...
if only he would allow his hand to remain longer in mine.

Ex-Boyfriends (with Others), Sixteen Years On

Is there a term for this?
These conversations,
bright and deft from long-knowing,
with concern foregrounded,
convened once or twice a quarter.
Usually over the phone,
sometimes over a cup of coffee,
or more ambitiously,
a meal.
The sharing of the empirical—
books read, articles written,
talks given, clients guided.
Fine work completed,
miracles managed in these menacing times.
The family inquired after,
(relatively) good health celebrated,
this no minor feat,
propelled by a potpourri of pills imbibed daily,
the body under siege, but resilient yet,
the heart unblushing in the trenches
of anti-plague guerilla warfare.

So at ease I imagined myself, no—us—to be
that once I considered travel together,
to rejuvenate among literary friends in provincial X,
away from beaches and tourists,
to walk against whitewashed walls
and torrents of scarlet flowers
under heavens never before so blue
to sample plain yet fiery fare found far
from the market stalls in the village square.
Until there was mention of a native young man (or two),
lithe and keen,

who would surely stay in your room,
would not simply be spotted, to and fro, from behind curtains,
but would be part of the trip in ways, many unforeseen,
showered with tokens and trinkets and things,
and I thought of you standing over just such a young man,
arranging the arc of his ass,
having him with force and tenderness,
matters of mortality momentarily displaced,
and I scattered from the runway of this voyage,
with these images inscribed in this way,
so crumpled and distraught and unforgiving then was I.

On How the Other Half Lived

He had become a researcher of rejection,
a master of the mask of cheer.
Although eternally unmatched, friends would turn to him for
support at moments of romantic crisis. As if he would know!
Perhaps this was because he always had a stash of chocolates
and clichés handy, many of which, oddly enough,
involved animals—
there's more fish in the sea or
you've just got to get back on that horse or ...

The sociolinguists tell us that clichés endure for a reason,
he would pontificate, tissues materializing magically (if discreetly),
there's power in their pithiness.
But later he wondered whether he had correctly
remembered the clichés or whether their threads
had in fact unraveled on the icicles of his own numbness.
At other times, he would offer a bibliography of folk ballads or
love-gone-awry poems or even anthologies of them.
You really are such a resource, they effused.

Having performed such diligent service in the public good,
he was stunned into speechlessness when the roles were reversed.
The words that had so often been directed at him—
I just need some space or
No, it's not you, it's me or
You need to find someone who can give you what you need or,
worst of all, let's be friends—
seemed more measly than ever when he turned to use them.
Suddenly, he was ill-prepared.

Nowhere could he locate the armor, not against,
but for the other. He had become the unbearable—the catalyst to
anguish, the perpetrator of the paralysis of sad sack/gloom-and-
doom-dom. And yet something had to be done.
If only there were some sort of intermediate method
(if not a half-way measure) between language and silence,
that would neither mollify nor muffle nor render immobile,
a hand extended to acknowledge impossibility and to offer assurance.
His friends, once the counseled, insisted there was.

Bisexuality (of Sorts), or,
Rabbinical Compromise Unearthed

Set aside the strapping man,
his intoxicating musky scents,
the biceps that could present you to the heavens
(for there is always interest there),
the weight of him that could crush you down to oblivion
(we won't field the question of interest there),
the glory of him so lauded by the Greeks and their followers,
who not so incidentally sought to seduce us with their sirens and statues,
and to derail us, leaving us stranded from our one true mission,
a fleshly glory whose specific manifestations I shall not elucidate here,
for Torah time is of the essence,
we shall not waste.
Rather, set aside the possibility of him,
yet retain still his image,
sculpted in the Divine.

For here now is another that tempts you not at all,
fruit equally lustrous, yet so differently chiseled
precisely for you that you may serve the Lord our God.
A softer but nonetheless resilient presence who will remain
in sickness and in health, who will bring forth your likeness
and perhaps even likenesses with the Lord our God's will
in a flawed but successful union
of service and devotion offering to our nation a link in the eternal chain
perhaps someday love even if never desire,
although for that you may dip into your stockpile of impossibility
relegated now to your heart's netherest regions.
This presence will not fail you.
Even as you should and must choose her, remember
you need not forsake him entirely.
In obscurity's light, his phantom, still strapping, may also remain.

Early Talkie

Here we are; look see us.
The forces in the world
arrayed against this possibility,
plush with lashes, prisons, beheadings,
hangings, hard labor, stonings,
and verses fluorescent across centuries,
have been unable to prevent this culmination.

Look at you with your lips unwavering towards mine.
Listen to you reciting words whose meaning
I recognize but cannot fathom.
What know I of this kind of love?
Your arms gather me up as if I am of goose down,
when I am only goosey with you, your refusal to let history define us,
your ax ahack in this thicket of tumult.

Let the hyenas snicker outside;
let the mob with Book in fist cry out in impotence.
They too are welcome.
They shall merely enhance our merry say you.
No one else shall enter here your beard whispers.
My cock shall enter you, biblically or not;
you shall not elude me.

All shall hear and see and therefore know.
There I've said it,
you chuckle further into the lens:
Unplug your ears;
the sound shall not go mute.
Feast your eyes;
the camera shall not pan away.

Utopia

Come unto me. Don't dim the lamp.
Let me beam upon your breasts.
The compartments of your trunk shall be unpacked—
here bulbous, there concave, everywhere vast.
By all means, do giggle as I trace the atlas of furry ruddy,
the curlicues and honeycombs of mottled.

Come unto me. Unwrap yourself.
Let me nibble on this plenty.
I will raise your belly to lavish your sex gleaming far below.
Let me lick the swirl, the cream delectable beneath.
You may mock the glut of my metaphor,
but do not underestimate the resolve of my finger tips.

Come to me. Let go the "unto." Look not downward.
This is who you are; this is who you have become.
Remember not now the youth at the windows high above
with their sting and laughter and tomatoes.
These eyes shall not turn away.
You are here at last. The eviction notices have been rescinded.

Trains Passing in the Railroad Apartment

Once my father came to visit me,
the only family member ever to have done so
in the more than twenty years since my exodus.
He slipped past my Italian landlady sitting sentry without a second look.
Perhaps his long beard and black coat in summer scorch
set something ablaze in her, having to do with robes swishing
from rooms murky with moans for repentance
down alleyways into the piazza, pigeons rising in outrage,
stirring something altogether enormous and familiar,
despite the difference in tradition. Perhaps.
She, not given to reserve, never mentioned it. I'll never know now.

As he passed through my *mezuzah*-less doorway, I wondered whether
Father's purity would cleanse, or at least elevate, the impurity here.
Or would the reverse take place?
I so wanted him to feel, if not comfortable,
then at least not implausible in this setting.
I had debated for weeks which posters to take down for his visit.
Is Vermeer's *Girl Wearing Turban* as improper as the outline
of the nude woman on the Chez Panisse 1977 Garlic Festival?
The sages, after all, forbid glancing at even
the smallest finger of a woman.
Could the maiden of modesty be exempted?

What about the prohibition on graven images? I had considered hiding
some of the books, but ultimately decided against it.
There were simply too many, nearly all appalling in some way.
Where would I put the acres of them?
Besides, who did I think I was fooling?
Certainly not Father, who reclined on the green chair,
his back turned against both young ladies in question,
his fedora and coat on the ottoman

salvaged from the Housing Works Thrift Shop.
After he declined fruit and nuts, the food offerings
I had thought to be least affected by the laws of *kashrut*,

Father elaborated, with characteristic elegance,
on a passage in the weekly Torah portion. I wish I had taken notes.
Even then I knew this was an event worthy of documentation.
But for once the Torah seemed to have failed Father.
He soon asked to lie down.
I guided him to the windowless bedroom in my railroad apartment,
our roles momentarily reversed.
I landed in the front room, swaying by the window,
peering down on my landlady on the stoop,
my knuckles white from not-trembling,
my eyes red from not-weeping.

Day of Unrest

I.

Father implores me to return:
there's so much for you here.
Here are texts for you to savor, words to align a life.
Here are elders who have handed you the keys to a treasure
transcendent of time and place.
All that you seek can be found here.
There is no need to look further.
At the Wailing Wall I entered the wailing
to will your return out of ancient stone.
In the long winter of our diaspora,
I pray for you daily and only that you will keep the Sabbath.
My pleading directly to you is therefore only part of a broader regimen.
A place is set at the table for you, alongside that of the prophet Elijah.
You will be welcomed in his eternal embrace.

II.

My friend implores me to discontinue the dialogue.
Your father can never visualize the path you have taken. For him,
you have simply strayed from the "one true" one, namely his.
He can never see you in your becoming and having become and
becoming anew. All the ways of the no-longer-new you are
beyond the pale. But it's been more than a generation.
It's time to disentangle from this dyad,
to fashion yourself as someone other than an eternal yang
trapped in a conflict whose goalposts never budge.
You are more than the embodiment of expectations unmet,
dreams devastated (if not beyond repair). Yes, we all have our histories,
but the strategy of foregrounding is yours to devise. Step back from
the portrait of absence, this empty frame. Your Saturdays belong
to you. Know that you are welcome here with us. For now.

III.

The Sabbath bride chants my name, draping the lace of her veil
of not-imploring around my heaving shoulders.
Hand-sewn by my grandmother not far from Lublin, she says.
It is tear-resistant by now, she assures me. Welcome.
Here is the tranquility granted by God.
This day shall be ours. All of this is yours. We slow dance together,
my fingers admiring the small of her back, the skill of her step.
But the Torah calls out to us. We proceed to the weekly portion,
how Abraham and Sarah were blessed late with a child.
Even as I conjure that ancient rejoicing,
I can't help but wonder if I too will be blessed thus in old age.
Don't our sages command us to apply sacred texts to our own lives?
The Sabbath bride does not respond,
leading me instead to the feast now outspread before us.

IV.

Smiling, I think of the man on the subway who winked at me as I exited the train, imagining licking this couscous from his fingers. I know he too would not have been immune to its delights or those of its provider. What is the connection of couscous to lace from Lublin? Suddenly Father appears, stern of gaze, and in his Sabbath finery, imposing in dress. Is this an interruption of my fantasy or a part of it? I realize that the threads of my dream are getting tangled on the spokes of the loom of rest. Father assumes the helm as is his wont, commanding the Sabbath bride to address the tendrils that have escaped from her veil. The Sabbath bride only smiles. Without asking (and without protest on our part), she gathers us closer into the veil's folds and the intoxication of her perfume.
As my eyelids begin to lower, I glimpse Father's white beard traipsing over her satin sleeves and feel his body trembling alongside mine.

Lush

It's two over. Well, not exactly.
It's actually around the corner,
but visible catty (!)-corner.
Through the tree-tall weeds and over
the smaller ones of my next-to-door neighbor's yards,
the Eminent Domain gleams grayly.

The patriarch tends to the tidiness of things:
the shrubs manicured, branches pruned, lawns mowed.
Under a massive, floppy sunhat, the matriarch tucks the petunias
into their beds and croons to the geraniums on the patio's ledge.
Sometimes she pauses in her work to stroke the orange tomcat,
whose purring seems softer only than the house's own.

Their children, of college-ish age,
lounge languidly on lawn chairs or on an ornamental bench,
sometimes with a novel, sometimes with a magazine.
How should I know?
On special summer Saturday evenings,
candles in white bags line the terrace and yard.

Several lanterns enhance the festivity.
Ice cubes tinkle against crystal; liquid is lavished freely.
Long past midnight there are chimes of conversation
on places visited, courses completed, professors be/rated.
Sometimes a tease, followed a giggle of mock protestation.
Spencer, if you don't stop right now ... !

There is nothing apparently sinister or innocuous here,
merely lives lived
and observed through a bathroom window yards away.
Could this be Greenwich, Connecticut?
Have I landed on the border of a John Cheever story
only to be denied access to customs?

The nude neighboring behind the naked bathroom window
never figures into their orbit.
How could he? Why should he?
Beyond their tableau, beyond this poem,
he lurks uninvited, another spectator in the city in search of sleep,
green eyes wide green with **** in an herb-garden green bathroom.

Birdwatching Without Binoculars

I did not survive the culture war(s) unscathed.
Quite the contrary.
In fact, some say I have post-traumatic stress disorder.
Others counter such claims.
Apparently it's not like being pregnant. Hmm ...
Why don't we work to uncover the trajectory of things, they propose,
how the blessing of night has come to elude you,
how you catapulted supine onto this gangplank.

Years of finessing the same basic arguments to indifferent or
hostile ears have taken their toll, I respond.
Even back then, I wondered if I was changing minds, but I felt I had to
remain a combatant, that I could not leave the trenches, that there was
necessarily honor in my battle. Isn't that what the young did?
Perhaps I also felt that the powers of my argumentation were being
honed amidst the barrage returned at me, that in the dodging of volleys
I was somehow becoming limber and loose.

But the staccato of my step only led to new questions.
Despite my determination on various fronts—home, school, barricade—
whom had I reached, let alone taught? Would I ever know?
And where once I thought a truce had been declared,
I now understood otherwise. The rhetoric that once was has returned,
more virulent than ever. I see that this war has not
ended, that perhaps it may never. Is war inherently finite?
If it has no end, is it something other than war?

Enough of these pontifications, their eyes declaim even as they
listen politely. How does this make you *feel?* If the personal is political,
is the political not also personal? I retreat from their prodding and
lean into the pane, spotting sparrows in trees. I once thought I could
escape into their world, or at least into scrutiny of it:
call, gray/brown, flight, streak. I too can detect and dissect. But the war
(or whatever this is) will not release me, and so I turn away, aware now
of blood dribbling on beige. This couch will have to be reupholstered.

Disgrace, Ongoing

differs from the interlude of disgrace—
the professor in fling with the co-ed,
with her tresses and her effervescence
and her ease with medieval French handwriting,
grasping at dazzle with vim newly-recovered
until the bureaucrats finally arrive on the scene.
The winds,
in their dampness and chill,
reassert sensibility.
October is restored.
The intellectual arranges his re-diminished world,
bruised by the contrast
between the silk-strewn bed
and the stone verdict of the tribunal.
The co-ed returns,
dazed,
to the path less-thistled,
to penmanship a little less loopy,
the fire of aging kisses lingering on her opal skin.

Disgrace, ongoing offers no such delineation.
Instead of a single sin,
the banished lives in infamy overflowing its banks.
He inhales the aromas of the bakery below,
with its rugelach and tortes, the life now off limits.
Here, time is measured not in moments crystalline,
but in swathes of muck, barely differentiated.
If the villagers can sometimes come to pardon
mad passion briefly descended,
there is no such generosity for the disgraced, ongoing.
Nor is there absolution from on high—no release granted
through a grate or over a lectern,
candles flickering in the background,

for there has been no repentance.
The disgraced, ongoing clings to the treason
that has catapulted him into these gray rooms,
with their marionettes shadowdancing at midday,
and, year-in, year-out, refuses the embrace of redemption or
the honey-drizzled approbation of the graced.

> *'Aśeret Yeme Teshuvah/Ten Days of Repentance 5772*

Secrets of Anaïs

Once I wrote a happy poem.
Not a contented poem,
if held at the right angle,
viewed under a carefully calibrated light.
Not a pleased poem, all things considered,
if I do say so myself.
But a happy poem, plain in its radiance.

I entered its corridors, feeling my way like a child walking
through the Giant Heart at the Franklin Institute
for the first time. I poked here and there, exhilarated by
the buoyancy of the walls. I slipped into sponginess.
Instead of kerplunk, whoosh! I knew I would not be chastised.
I let myself absorb the range of shade;
the colors of joy were too infinite to enumerate.

No books or maps were provided, as the guides stated at the outset.
Just allow yourself to roam, they advised, you can't get lost here.
I saw rain forest fruit floating in front. I stopped to sample.
Beige gorillas sipped iced chai drinks topped with mint. They
beckoned me over, winking, then suggested I join the flamingo
techno rave happening just around the corner. I delighted in the blush
and brush of their feathers against the vestiges of my melancholy.

I accepted all invitations;
declining was not even considered.
And I skipped onward; I shan't elaborate here on what I saw there.
A synopsis could not capture all that was revealed, then offered to me.
Besides, you get the idea. I did reach the poem's end
without mishap, just as the guides foresaw.
I said this rejoicing is mine and is now yours, ours.

But I didn't know what to do once outside the poem.
The guides had refused my parting present per policy.
As delighted in my company
as the gorillas had been, they seemed equally so
when I looked back on them en route to departure.
Would they wish to sustain contact?
Had I missed an essential cue?

Anaïs from the millinery would know. Of that I was sure.
Suddenly I yearned to see what concoctions were now featured in the
windows of her boutique so out of the way. How ever does she get by?
I wanted to hear how the rounded lilt of her syllables heightened the
pointedness of her observations. Besides, a new chapeau was in order.
This one was battered by the adventures outlined above.
Once I almost wrote a happy poem.

In Musical Limbo(s)

I.

There is no campfire here,
no huddling in chill mountain air
with blankets and spirits and sparks disappearing into stars.
Instead, we come together where and when we can.
Sometimes a midday sing-a-long in a summer sun porch,
sometimes a new year's gathering,
sometimes a retirement celebration in a candlelit apartment.

We can't stay long from song, you see,
the ones with which most of us were not raised, which we did
not learn from mother crooning over crib or soothing our brow
over distress with which only she and song could dispel.
For only later did we learn these songs, this seemingly
bottomless trove on love, labor, lullaby, religion, and revolution.
But this time we forgot to make photocopies.

Instead, we pass around the single copy of the tattered book,
studying the lyrics, the notes, and the translations,
aching to master, to absorb into musical mind and song skin.
Those who can read notation are that much further along.
We turn to the one who knows these songs best. Even she falters.
It's been so long, and, despite regular attendance
at the annual language retreats, the maintenance so sporadic.

When the lyrics trail into unremembered,
we march on with melody. This too should not be discounted.
Next time we'll have the photocopies ready.
Mir zaynen klal-ṭuers/We are community activists. If there's a task at
hand, we can complete it. We have spent years expanding our knowledge.
We will claim what we never had, what we know is rightfully ours,
even as we know we have arrived so very late.

II.

We exit onto First Avenue,
borne along by the well-heeled hordes leaving the art cinema.
We consider the pacing, the plot, the performances,
the lighting, the costumes, the direction. Our scalpels are sharp,
yet we are not parsimonious with praise.
We are pleased that our attention was held, our expectations met;
for some, even surpassed. Where to now?

It's no longer undiscovered, hipsters of all ages abound now.
Still there's something about this next place that we love.
It shouldn't be hard to figure out. There's much to admire.
The potato pierogis are always just so; the borscht doesn't lack charm.
The comely wait staff, some from our ancestral homelands, provide that
something-something. We're not above that, you know. Perhaps it's all
of these things; perhaps it's none of them; perhaps just because it's ours.

We land in a bar devoted to the music from the crossroads, not far
from the ravages of recent genocide. Supermodels and bodybuilders
and dandies-on-the-prowl abound but so do scholars and devotees of
music so intoxicating everyone has to slither and shimmy. The strands
from many lands converge in this perfumed perspiring room.
The belly dancer smiles and sways, the tinkle of her bells audible
above the clapping and choreographed frenzy encircling her.

We stumble back into night. One of us begins a melody.
It is Friday night, after all.
The candles lit by our families in neighborhoods not far from here
have long gone out. We join in, excavating remembered phrases,
and not just those from the first stanza.
One dazzles with her harmonies, rich with flourish.

If only we could sing like this more often.
If only our families could hear our song, led by women.
If only we could integrate this music
as we learned it so long ago, but with our twists today.
We can, we say.
Perhaps we will. *Guṭ Shabes̀*/a good Sabbath to you. *A guṭn Shabes̀*.

Editor's Edict, or, Bowed by Absence

She said, "*A poem has to stand on its own.*
It should not need a glossary."
So here goes.
This will be a poem without signage of any kind:
turn here for the meaning of x,
squat here to discover a hint into y.

In vain will you scour for
aspects of otherness revealed or repressed.
You cannot help but crave these assurances;
you have become accustomed to them.
Allow your fingers, however they may tremble,
to grope the walls, jagged in their flatness.
There will be bandages on hand should they get bloodied.

Be sure not to stumble over those pesky etymological speed bumps.
Make your way down the linoleum-tiled corridor
past the locked doors to the shuttered windows.
You will wonder where they might have lead.
The squeak of your sneakers will announce your "unencumbered" tread.
You will have just managed to skirt
the ungainliness of translation, it seems,
the burden of the asterisk, the heartbreak of approximation.

You did so want to mediate.
You can't shake the daydream of yourself as diplomat
with banter and enigmatic expression
beneath sputtering sconces amidst winter coats slowly donned.
How do you say "shucks" in the hovering tongue?
Your eyes water in the uniformity of it all.
Just beyond your vision field, willow branches sweep
a plain of nearly forgotten diminutives once thought quaint.
Ever so faintly, a gray tomcat sniffs a clump of steaming colloquialisms.

Anxiously, you reach for the bi-lingual dictionary.

On Being a Minorities Poet

Your poems are too gay
    Your poems are too universal
        Your poems are too sexual
            Your poems are too squeamish
Your poems are too Jewish
    Your poems are too assimilationist
        Your poems are too religious
            Your poems are too worldly
Your poems are too Yiddish-y
    Your poems are too translated
        Your poems are too accessible
            Your poems are too elusive
Your poems are too ornate
    Your poems are too austere
        Your poems are too emotional
            Your poems are too intellectual
Your poems are too political
    Your poems are too decadent
        Your poems are too scandalous
            Your poems are too tame
Your poems are too self-absorbed
    Your poems are too socially aware
        Your poems are too heavy
            Your poems are too blithe
Your poems are too flat
    Your poems are too sparkly
        Your poems are too narrative
            Your poems are too character-driven
Your poems are too dialectic
    Your poems are too polyphonic
        Your poems are too dissonant
            Your poems are too smooth

Your poems lack variety
      Your poems lack cohesion
            Your poems are too monochromatic
                  Your poems are too gaudy
Your poems are too old-fashioned
      Your poems are too experimental
            Your poems are too prose-y
                Your poems are too ...
No, what I really want to say is this:

Have you considered writing short stories?

Proofreading, or, You Could Just Hire Someone for This Part, You Know

I. The Hunt

The mulch has borne fruit.
Profusion, no longer indistinct, has rewarded my persistence.
Only now I must scan for weeds,
rather, the snags in the foliage.
The tools have been sharpened—the blade for cutting,
the shears for sprucing, the sigh for exasperation.
Against the clink and clank of this equipment,
I stumble through these fields that I thought I knew
(my own, after all)—
here, aqua tea roses;
there, around that small bend, a bed of desert ferns.
A panorama of improbable glitter,
of nature harnessed to the imperative of coherence.
Each time I envision clarity, I pause.
A shirt tears; skin is cerated.
Merely nicks, these, I assure myself—to be eradicated in due time.
My relief is wary of joy. Surely, the leaves are not rustling.

II. The Aftermath

The gates are now open.
A sign with the word "Display has been discreetly posted.
A group of tourists trickle in.
Their gestures are measured, writ miniature.
Some poke; others prod. The more adventurous lift and shake.
There are murmuring sounds;
all are careful to veer from exclamation.
I try to choreograph these comings-and-goings,
the hushed assessment.
But a force beyond politeness has been unleashed.

My tools are of no use now.
The smudged horizon, the pallid clusters are suddenly quite apparent.
Despite all my care, signs of carelessness glow in neon.
Looking around, I pray others won't notice
or will at least pretend they don't.
As if the eyes of the lion would miss the limping zebra,
as if the limping zebra could avoid the lion's jaw.

Eavesdropping

This is some of what can be found in a book:
who owned it: from the library of ... , the signing,
the shapes of the scrawl, the ardor vibrating in the dedication:
for Dorothea, in fond remembrance of our sojourn in Bratislava
and, as if in Morse code, the notes of others:
Tell Bruno to bring home the bacon!

This is some of what can be left in a book:
store receipts (especially the handwritten ones from the vintage shops)
doctor's prescriptions Chinese fortune cookie maxims plumber bills
the phone number of the man in the shadows of an East Village dive bar
the photo of the ex with PFLAG moms at a Pride parade
the after-hours pass still so crisp to visit Mother in the hospital

This is some of what can be felt on a book:
the red and yellow ink hovering just above the margins of its pages
the fingers that smudged caressed the corners and passed it
on and on until it arrived in this antiques mart off the interstate
delivered to me skepticism measured weighed until finally
banished by the fact of these words cosseted this object discovered

the fragrances of fellowship in the 24-hour diner
care for a refill, hon
the disappearance of sugar cube into freshly-brewed elixir
as the crowd files in for the bars have finally let out
whatever *are* the no-longer baby dykes wearing these days
the waitresses returning the flirt

the plot argument rhythm music that cannot be set aside for all this
ruckus so sweet the dénouement revealed conversion confirmed in
the contentment of the reader framed Hopperesquely in the plate window
born of these words framed thus in the unhurried turning of page
in the hard hats overalls the arrival can it be already
of the early morning construction worker shift

the silt scattering from gingerly opened covers years later
pottery fragments from a classical era
the unbinding of manuscript splinters from
the (almost musty) binding of accepted truth
hieroglyphics you will have to master some day
come now gather and decipher

Luddite's Exhortation

When you open a book, any book, a century or more from now,
if there are even books then,
if the words "avid" and "reader" are still paired with regularity,
if you can be brought to put aside the gadgets with their glow
and the links luring you, *clickety-clack*, ever elsewhere, ever beyond,
when you happen upon this book, neither fetish object nor artifact,
in a remainders bin, (there will surely always be those),
worn, crumbling into a blizzard
in your jittery hands, if ...

Remember that this was chosen as backdrop:
mother-of-pearl, egg shell, ivory, or even saffron ...
and this as fabric:
leafy, grainy, speckled, veined or ...
and this as font:
spindly, sturdy, old style, or antiqua ...
and that this photograph was retrieved from the millions
on a stock site or rescued mangled from a telephone pole or that this
illustration was spotted, among cappuccinos, in an out-of-the-way café.

Remember that these tones were deemed
to star best opposite these images, these words;
that for all the errors found too late,
hundreds of others were snared.
Remember that for all that this book did emerge,
countless others did not. *Cup that absence.*
Forget not the editor who responded to countless missives
on these and other urgencies from a belief in
the power of words arranged just so, out of, dare we say, *joy*.

Remember s/he who penned the words,
the letters chiseled to maximum effect, who insisted that they
have a place in the world beyond napkin or notebook or screen,
as the whoosh of the night shift whistle scattered,
as the infant's cries faded, as the lover's snores commenced,
as the world begrudged approbation or wagged its finger
or thundered its indifference,
as stars caressed the tendrils framing the mind's irises,
as the moon lowered its awnings over day into respite.

On your tottering shelves, a sliver of space for this one.

How the Peeping Tom Came to Remember

The staircase is indeed graceful,
delicately forging a sense of anticipation.
No one will be pushed down it over a will contested.
Diamonds and other gems flicker in subdued settings.
Women are clad in gowns of hushed hues
in fabric cut in simple, sumptuous lines.
Here and there—a flash whirls by,
a socially sanctioned splotch of madcap.

Men cradle their companions' elbows proudly,
nodding at the right moments and to the right people.
There are no beads of perspiration here.
Perhaps it is the air conditioning,
purring inaudibly, orchestrating its alchemy.
Or perhaps it is the sense of entitlement borne with breeze:
Of course we are fabulous.
Until proven otherwise, we will assume the same of you.

Without any apparent signal the movement slows
and then ceases altogether.
Individuals ascend to the podium to declaim their
word concoctions to eyes willed unblinking
and (finally occasionally) sagging heads.
Here and there,
a gilded coiffure is fingered and reassembled;
flowered fans flutter.

As he peers through the window in the door,
having somehow eluded the bouncer,
the words from a long-ago note, bordered too in gilt,
flutter across a pastry puff (at least that) snatched
from a platter whisked along by a waiter:
"*Your words too could (almost) be recited in polite society.*
But with a few ill-advised phrases,
with an insistence on filth, you ruin it all."

Fingers Beneath the Gavel

What precisely is the nature of the transgression, he inquired.
The Sabbath is to be abided, sure;
the dietary laws are to be heeded, too.
And yet I know you delight in Saturday picnics by the lake
and Sunday bacon (so singular in its ways of wafting)
only slightly less than its crunch and flavor.
You are free to follow or flout as you wish.
This is not (yet) a theocracy.

What precisely is the nature of the wrongdoing, he asked.
Prayer with a quorum is mandated;
the sacred texts, with their commentaries, yearn to be mastered.
And yet I know you skirt the houses of worship with their curious eyes
and the study halls whose argumentation no longer seduces.
You are free to pore over novels and verse, your eternal distractions,
to revel in your intellectual promiscuity in the city library at evening.
You will not be jailed.

What precisely is the nature of the sin, he asked.
The verse is too well-known to be cited here;
its meanings too often debated and disregarded.
I know how you seek to sequester yourself from its power
even as you swallow and bend and open to wallow in its desecration.
You are free to hunt and to cram the void you yourself fashioned
with flesh and touch and chimera of the most appalling kind.
You will not find comfort there or here.

The precise nature of the heresy lies just outside all of this, he explained. You imagine that, despite all of the offenses outlined above, you shall be rewarded or lauded or at least granted a berth in the world-to-come, the true world everlasting. That through your concocted code of observance, you have somehow made good. That in your lack of repentance, in your brazenness, necessarily obscure, you shall be accepted.
This is the ultimate failing.
This is your heresy.

A Meditation on the Question of Agency

How did the heretic land on this rickety footstool,
cowering before the junkies near Sabbath's end while others
celebrate the movement victories. He gazes at the letters that have
fluttered in from those transfixed by the model of his hereticism,
yet who have chosen a different path,
or rather to remain on the one they all once shared.
He stares blankly at the postmarks and the scrawled invitations
for meetings, with their curiosity and need.

Against the cacophony of coffee machines, these have not gone well.
There are claims made, criticisms leveled.
It is suggested that he compose on other topics: on - or - , for instance.
The heretic is exhorted to "get perspective" and "lighten up"
for this is a free country.
The flames of the auto-da-fe do not lick at his heels.
The hangman's noose does not hover here,
as it does elsewhere.

And then there are the offerings from those reared in milder environs.
From them the questions are posed:
what have you done, *what will you now that you are no longer caged?*
Rather than dwell, it is felt that he should incorporate all that is best
from his not-quite-former world into his currently evolved self.
He has the power to fashion a confident yet rooted persona.
Wear what you wish, but avoid labels and fixed identities.
Know that, in fact, you are not a heretic, they contend.

The heretic does not answer or dismiss these criticisms, questions, and contentions, none of which are, after all, unreasonable.
Not from restraint or stoicism, but in deference to the quiet not yet his. Having mastered the praxis of flight, liberation remains for him an abstraction. No longer on the footstool, he now stands in the center of the circle of stones on the brink of being cast while reaching for the embrace of the departing Sabbath queen.
A crow peers forth from his quivering, serrated throat.

Passover 5772

The Spectacle of Spinoza's Specs

He thought to prepare for this poem with supplementary reading—
biographies and such—to move beyond the image
of the philosopher in ex-communicado,
grinding optical lenses as glass dust drifted deep into his body.
He thought to consult the sketches in the lexicons and encyclopedias
of the ones who abandoned the study halls
and the synagogues for another kind of argumentation
and direct action leading all too often to prison and deportation.

He thought to prepare for this poem by entering the mine, braving its
dust and the walls with his yarmulke lamp and his soft bookish hands.
He would study the details of their lives, he thought: how they read their
first forbidden words, then passed them secretly to avoid the
punishment beyond measure, how a particular holiday melody
pleased them, how apple trees flowered against blue knolls,
how they knew they would ache for these shapes and scents even
as they departed just after midnight. No, even in the midst of departure.
He did so think this. And he had the books piled close by in readiness.

He would hold these lives under the light, as he did with words,
examining them for line and luster. He thought that his
diligence would be rewarded with dialogues cleverly rendered with these
antecedents, that their model would lend perspective to his rooms with
their books and bills and dust of a more quotidian kind.
He remembered when he used terms like "rigorous" and "thorough"
not exactly glibly, but certainly without reticence. Only now he steps
away from them, from the books unread, and strolls instead along the
canal. Sticky condoms drift alongside, buoyed by its apparent calm.

Even in exile, he was almost a good student.

Thorns of Perhaps

Perhaps this shall save him

he who has not crossed a synagogue threshold in years
except for a bar mitzvah or ... or as a memoirist delighted
by the sensation on skin of melody etched into wood
prayer shawl golding under sun into binding gilded
the sting of belonging and yet not

Perhaps this shall save him

he who has not submerged in sacred text in decades
except the one by he who brimstoned against gossip and worldly learning
and that largely to please Father may he thrive until 120
years of gridlock crackling between them along the phone wire
relieved that he could weep unseen into indifferent pages

Perhaps this shall save him

he who has not sought out a sanctioned meal in years
except when required by the customs of visitors
or when visiting others startled by a primal animal pleasure
in these stews and breads and flaking curlicued pastries in his palate's
evocation of a clearly demarcated place in the tribal order

Perhaps this shall save him

he who decodes daily the secrets the dates of release buried in
verse the many works using the same title or entwined gasping
as they obsess over the female body as he has never
the very authorship of these insights as if unnecessary given the garland
of honorifics the teacher the sainted one the most glorious how holy is he

Perhaps this shall save him

he who differentiates this one from others identically named
he who follows up using the phone number on the title page verso
accent in the mother tongue indeterminate unsettling evoking the pious
and the profane the familiarity with the whip elaborating on what must be
done so that their words may endure he the most unlikely of guides

Perhaps this shall save him by this it is meant

this toil joyous

fingers and wrists wailing after years of motion seemingly repetitive
in this box not dissimilar from countless others
but distinguished by a tiny flame flickering eternally above
and a singed burgundy velvet curtain slightly parted
against the fires that rage just out of sight but never far away

Dialectic in Abeyance

With little direction from their teacher,
the children—boys in white shirts and blue shorts,
girls in white blouses and blue plaid jumpers,
both genders united by navy blue knee socks—
file tidily up the stone stairs, presumably into the sanctuary,
out of view of the heretic loitering across the street, in any case.

The children are being schooled in the intricacies of submission.
They will remember these outings: the break from the classroom,
these homilies and sermons, their own links in the chain of tradition.
They will remember the candles in daylight and, with eyes lowered,
the rhythm of call and response: knowing what to say when.
They will remember the palace of certainty shielding the unknowable.

Children of the uncertain or the unbelieving, on the other hand,
will have no such collective memory, reflects the heretic.
They will not have entered edifices constructed long ago to celebrate
a force unseen, to sing hymns to events that may not have happened,
all the while rejoicing in the flutter of the dark
that will soothe away the summer and the dust of doubt.

Even if they arrive here later in life,
children of the uncertain or the unbelieving will never have had
this foundation, the ease of assumed understanding.
They will have to work harder to master these arcana, to submit,
for they have not learned through precepts bequeathed by elders.
Their missteps in the labyrinth, along with their zeal, will be noted.

They may find themselves longing for the ways of their parents, the mess of uncertainty and unbelieving. They may remember arguments at the kitchen table, figures gesticulating on a soapbox, reason marshaled to question authority, action direct with a placard or an editorial or bodies. Perhaps he will see these children some day outside a lecture or labor hall or a bathhouse, thinks the heretic, turning finally away.

Briefly, they could swap stories from opposite sides of the heretical fence.

The Dirty Laundry Poem

Even if a thread commendable can somehow be salvaged
from your venom spewed against our sages
and against our mobile treasure glorious and everlasting,
even if all that you delineate on your path,
(I won't say moan or whine) on the pebbles in your shoes,

do you have to do it here, here for all to see,
here where our enemies can observe and rejoice
on our "backwardness" and "fanaticism" using it to nurture
the flowers of their enmity which have flourished
just fine without your help so no thank you very much.

Even if you choose to continue
with this so-called calling of yours,
with its accusations skimpily veiled,
even if you persist in risking not simply your own soul
but the very safety of our people,

remember that there are those who still and once love/d you,
who sustained you when you were powerless,
an infant naked in the noonday sun,
remember the hands veined speckled knobby that caressed
your sobbing fists, your thrashing limbs.

Even if this mnemonic device fails, and we expect it will, we remind you
that there are other means. Something has to be done. Listen, we know
who you are. For all your prancing and preening, you're a savvy faggot.
So strip off the finery and step away from the velvet rope.
You will not be told again.

Credo

Are you getting religious in your old age
wondered recently my ex-boyfriend he whose lips and cock and ...
are now inaccessible to me guarded by a no-trespassing sign
and pit bulls for despite years of spanking
I am still unable to resist shiny objects

If by religious you mean am I filled with
awe at the forests that still sustain our planet
the life infinitesimal and vast that flits between and through its green
fury at the forces that seek to diminish it all for gain
gratitude to those who risk for rescue

If by religious you mean am I filled with
awe at the miracle of a life born
the specificity of twinkle and crease and smile and outstretched fist
horror at the bullets budget cuts machetes swoosh the sales into ...
gratitude to those who see her schooled in a manner just and enduring

If by religious you mean am I filled with
awe at the rendition of a sonata a soliloquy on a dimly-lit stage
or the boulevards of Budapest and Buenos Aires
even as I consider the horrors that happened there not so long ago
and am grateful for the grace the precision of their grandeur evokes

If by religious you mean am I filled with
awe at the prayers that were instilled with devotion that I still remember
with their delineation of all that is possible
horror no confusion as they remain unanswered as if insufficient
gratitude for Sabbath melodies that return to me uninvited at rallies and ...

If by religious you mean am I filled with
awe at our shared love so flecked with amber and romp that it once was
despite the past and the future that would not recede
horror at our seemingly unstoppable desecration of the sacred
gratitude that you somehow in whatever way are still with me

Then I shall say yes I always have been even before I heard
Maria Callas' call or saw Ida Kaminska[1] flickering in the dark
even before I walked the mountains and byways of this land or exited
its borders to waltz over those of others even if I sleep in on Saturday yes
I am and yes I invite you to stop by bring the signage and those dogs
there is no time assigned for prayer the sanctuary never closes

---

1 — Ida Kaminska (1899-1980): star of the Yiddish theater and the 1965 film *The Shop on Main Street*

Way Stations Along the Via Dolorosa

I.

There is an apartment that is so familiar to me
that I gasp upon entry.
It could be Brighton Beach or Rockville or Petaḥ Tiḳvah or ...
Perhaps I am collecting papers for the scientific institute—
the minutes of long-ago meetings of immigrants
assembled on still alien sands.
Perhaps I am chatting with a pioneering librarian
alone near the end in assisted-living,
the cadences of the immigrant caretakers and the clatter of wheelchairs
the backdrop for our musings on the future of libraries.
Perhaps I am visiting the poet flooded by sun,
undeterred by dwindling readership,
with his wife fluttering exquisitely all around,
(gazpacho and indeterminate organic nibbles in hand),
yet bleak in his pronouncements on the withering of
our minority language into a poetless abyss.

II.

There is an apartment that is so familiar to me
that I shiver upon entry.
It could be Lakewood or Monsey or Bene Beraḳ or ...
Perhaps my hands are trailing the golden binding of the Tanakh and
Talmud and the equally gilded commentaries they have spawned.
Perhaps I am trying to avoid the eyes of the rabbis
scowling down upon me in disappointment
or those of the brides and grooms in the wedding portraits
or those of their offspring, fingers in the eye of Hitler's delirium.
Perhaps I am fingering the aroma of the Sabbath feasts to come,

flowering under the focus of the rabbi's wife,
yearning for her to step away from the hearth, however briefly,
to undo the taffeta of her modesty, to heed my call
whispered between her kerchief and unjeweled ear:
Come let us sit and listen to this convergence—our breathing in unison,
the alchemic bubble of your *tsholnt*/Sabbath stew,
the unfurling of the red carpet escorting the Sabbath Queen to her throne.
Bo'i kalah/Come, my bride.

III.

There is an apartment that is so familiar to me
that I smile upon entry.
It could be West Hollywood or Chelsea or Tel Aviv or …
Perhaps I am admiring a mid-century Danish modern sofa
or an arched metal floor lamp sure to be an original
or sneaking a peek at the
commemorative poster of the "Russia!" exhibition at the Guggenheim
as I carefully sip iced, hopefully undrugged, water
and await his emergence.
Perhaps I am avoiding the averted gaze of the Bruce Weber models,
wondering how it is I got to be here anyway,
here on worn knee, wrists bent, numb.
Perhaps I am offering a benediction on the abundance of his biceps,
rejoicing in the precision of his torso,
the orders quietly shouted, steeling myself to gaze no further
than the outline of his splendor in this violet shadow.

IV.

There is an apartment that is so familiar to me
that I exhale upon entry.
It could be Poncey-Highlands or Washington Heights or Brookland or ...
Perhaps the invitations of street walkers rend the night.
Perhaps the neighbors are assembling for a vigil
for the shopkeeper murdered nearby at Second Day of Christmas dusk,
as the flames of their cries lick the gaping windows of the apartment.
Perhaps I am again on the floor, only this time prostrate
leafing through a book of short stories
about the early plague years
gazing up at the towers of volumes,
(smiling on he, who not so long ago, had granted me this one,
uninscribed, with urgency and certainty and love),
stunned that, in spite of all of this,
in spite of all the danger into which I have placed my body,
I am somehow still here.

.IV

פֿאַראַן אַ דירה וואָס איז מיר אַזוי באַקאַנט
אַז איך אָטעם ווען איך קום אַרײַן.
סע וואָלט געקענט זײַן פֿאַנסי-הילאַנדס אָדער וואַשינגטאָן-הײטס אָדער ברוקלאַנד אָדער ...
אפֿשר רײַסן די פֿאַרבעטונגען פֿון די זונות אויף דער נאַכט.
אפֿשר פֿאַרזאַמלען זיך די שכנים אויף אַ וואָך
פֿאַרן קרעמער דאָ נישט ווײַט דערהרגעט געוואָרן בין-השמשות דעם צווייטן טאָג ניטל,
בשעת די פֿלאַמען פֿון זייערע געשרייען לעקן די גאַפֿנדיקע פֿענצטער פֿון דער דירה.
אפֿשר בין איך נאָך אַ מאָל אויפֿן דיל, נאָר דאָס מאָל געפֿאַלן כּורעים,
בלעטערנדיק אַ בוך דערצײַלונגען
ווגן די פֿרײַיִקע מגיפֿה-יאָרן
און קוק אַרויף אויפֿן ביכער-טורעם
(און דערמאָן זיך אין יענעם וואָס האָט מיר געגעבן אָט דאָס בוך,
אומגעאַכטמעט, אײליק, זיכער און מיט ליבע),
אין גאַנצן פֿאַרחידושט אַז, נישט געקוקט אויף אַלצדינג,
אויף דער סכּנה אין וועלכער איך האָב געשטעלט דעם גוף,
בין איך ווי עס איז נאָך אַלץ דאָ.

וועלכע בליִען אונטערן דער רביצינס אויגן,
און וואָס ווילן אַז זי זאָל אויעקגיין פֿונעם קאַמין קאַטש אויף אַ מאָמענט,
צעשפּיליִען דעם טאָפֿט פֿון איר צניעות, צו פֿאָלגן מײַן רוף
אַרײַנגעשושקעט צווישן איר טיכל און איר נאַקעטן אויער:
קום לאָמיר זיצן און זיך צוהערן צו אָט דעם צונויפֿקום—אונדזער צוזאַמענאַטעמען,
דעם פֿאַרכּישופֿדיקן בלעזל פֿון איִער טשאַלענט,
דעם צעוויקלען זיך פֿונעם רויטן טעפּעך וואָס באַלייט די מלכּה שבת צו איר כּיסא-הכּבֿוד.
באי כּלה, באי כּלה.

III.

פֿאַראַן אַ דירה וואָס מיר איז אַזוי באַקאַנט
אַז איך שמייכל ווען איך קום אַרײַן.
סע וואָלט געקענט זײַן מערבֿ האַליוווּד אָדער טשעלסי אָדער תּל-אָבֿיבֿ אָדער ...
אפֿשר באַוווּנדער איך אַ דעניש-מאָדערנעם דיוואַן פֿון מיטן-יאָרהונדערט
אָדער אַ געבויגטע פּאָדלאָגע-לאָמף וואָס איז זיכער אַן אָריגינעל
אָדער איך כאַפּ אַ קוק אויף דעם
יובל-פּלאַקאַט פֿון דער "רוסלאַנד!"-אויסשטעלונג אין גוגענהיים
בשעת זײַער אָפּגעהיט זופּ איך געאײַזט און לאָמיר האָפֿן אומנאַרקאָטיקט וואַסער
און וואַרט ער זאָל אַרויסקומען.
אפֿשר מײַד איך אויס דעם אויעקגעדרייטן בליק פֿון די ברוס וועבער-מאָדעלן,
זיך פֿרעגנדיק ווי אַזוי איך בין טאַקע אַהערגעקומען,
דאָ אויף אויסגעריבענע קניִען, געלענקען געבויגענע, געליימטע.
אפֿשר מאַך איך אַ ברכה אויף דער שפֿע פֿון זײַנע אָרעם-מוסקלען,
זיך פֿרייענדיק אין דער פֿרעציזקייט פֿון זײַן טול,
די באַפֿאַלן געשריגן שטילערהייט, און איך באַפֿעסטיק זיך נישט צו קוקן ווײַטער
ווי פֿון די קאַנטורן פֿון זײַן פּראַכט אין אָט דעם וויִאָלעטענעם שאָטן.

בניני-מיקלט אויף דער וויא-דאָלאָראָסאַ

I.

פאראן אַ דירה וואָס איז מיר אַזוי באַקאַנט
אַז איך מוז כאַפן דעם אָטעם ווען איך קום אַרײַן.
סע וואָלט געקענט זײַן בריטאָן-ביטש אָדער ראָקוויל אָדער פּתח-תקווה אָדער ...
אפשר זאָמל איך דאָקומענטן פאַרן וויסנשאַפטלעכן אינסטיטוט:
די פּראָטאָקאָלן פון זיצונגען פון ווײַטן אַ מאָל פון אימיגראַנטן
פאַרזאַמלט אויף נאָך אַלץ פרעמדע זאַמדן.
אפשר שמועס איך מיט אַ ביבליאָטעקאַר אַ פּיאָניער
אַליין, נאָענט צום סוף אין אַ מושבֿ-זקנים,
די ריטעמס פון אימיגראַנטישע העלפערס און דער טומל פון רעדערשטולן
דעם הינטערגרונט צו אונדזערע שמועסן וועגן דער צוקונפט פון ביבליאָטעקן.
אפשר קום איך צו גאַסט צום פּאַטע פאַרפלייצט אין זון,
נישט געשטערט פון דעם וואָס זײַן לייענערשאַפט ווערט קלענער,
זײַן פרוי פלאַטערט גראַציעז אַהין און אַהער,
(און זי טראָגט *גאַזפּאַטשאָ* און ווער ווייסט וועלכע אָרגאַנישע נאַשערײַ אין האַנט),
און ער מיט וויסטע דעקלאַראַציעס וועגן אונדזער מינדערהייט-לשון
וואָס ווערט פאַרדאַרט אַרײַן אין אַ תהום אַן פאָעטן.

II.

פאראן אַ דירה וואָס איז מיר אַזוי באַקאַנט
אַז איך ציטער ווען איך קום אַרײַן.
סע וואָלט געקענט זײַן לייקוווּד אָדער מאָנסי אָדער בני ברק ...
אפשר גלעטן מײַנע הענט דעם גאָלדענעם אײַנבונד פונעם תנך און
גמרא און די פירושים, אויך באַגילדעט, וואָס זײַנען אַרויסגעוואַקסן פון זיי.
אפשר פרוּוו איך אויסצומײַדן די אויגן פון די רבנים
וועלכע קוקן קרום אַראָפּ אויף מיר מיט אַנטוישונג
אָדער די אויגן פון די חתן-כלהס אין די חתונה-פאָרטרעטן
אָדער די פון זייער נאָכוווּקס, אַ שטאָך אין די אויגן פון היטלערס פיבער.
אפשר פינגער איך דעם אַראָמאַט פון די שבת-סעודות קומעדיקע,

J. Edgar Song

Take me to the water
not the one surging into infinite
with its missions and imperatives
but to the one hushed and brackish
where no one dares to picnic or swim

Take me to the water
there I will smooth away the contortions
dispel the heels clicking down the corridor
contingents from afar insisting on the one true way
perspiration beginning to form

Take me to the water
there I will flee he with the files and folders
accusations so tidy so pointed
names and images on the verge of display
the contents of these many years reduced to a box on the floor

Take me to the water
there I will disrobe in the circle of witness
of those who too used to slink and shiver and now will enfold me
the pine needles will brush my nipples the night sun will not retreat
as the wet darkness rises in greeting

דזש. עדגער-געזאַנג

נעם מיך צום וואַסער
נישט צו דעם וואָס כוואַליעט אינעם אין-סוף אַרײַן
מיט זײַנע שליחותן און אימפּעראַטיוון
נאָר צו דעם פֿאַרשוויגן און בלאַטיק
ווו קיינער דערוועגט זיך נישט צו מאַכן אַ פּיקניק אָדער שווימען

נעם מיך צום וואַסער
דאָרט וועל איך אויסגלעטן די קרימען
פֿאַרטרײַבן די אַפּצאַסן וועלכע קנאַקן דורכן קאָרידאָר
פּאַרטיעס פֿון דער וויטנס וואָס שפּאַרן זיך אויף דעם איין און איינציקן וועג
שווײַג וואָס הייבט זיך אָן פֿאָרמירן

נעם מיך צום וואַסער
דאָרט וועל איך אַנטלויפֿן פֿון אים מיט די דאָסיעען און טעקעס
באַשולדיקונגען אַזוי ציכטיק אַזוי שפּיציק
נעמען און געשטאַלטן וואָס האַלטן בײַם אַרויסווײַזן זיך
דער אינהאַלט פֿון אָט די אַלע יאָרן רעדוצירט צו אַ קעסטל אויפֿן דיל

נעם מיך צום וואַסער
דאָרטן וועל איך זיך אויסטאָן אין אַן עדות-קרייז
פֿון די וועלכע פֿלעגן זיך אויך שלײַכן און ציטערן און איצט וועלן מיך אײַנהילן
די סאָסנע-נאָדלען וועלן קוים אָנרירן די אַפֿלען די נאַקטזון וועט זיך נישט צוריקציִען
בשעת דאָס נאַסע פֿינצטערניש הייבט זיך אויף מיך צו באַגריסן

137

Beach Glass Necklace

There are no carousels nearby, no children's laughter painted
in the hue and music of yesteryear.
There are no aromas of cotton candy and popcorn and taffy
to blunt the wind and wave and witness.
There are no prohibitions nailed to planks, no sentries posted
to denounce suspicious movement from a throne on high.

There are others around and about, to be sure.
And yet we don't think to assess theirs and ours and ours in relation
to theirs. We take step, as if we know, as if we've always known.
Eyes averted, we smile from within the glee of skin.
Umbrellas and chairs have been omitted. We will not be shielded;
the *terra infirma* of these sands are not ours to claim, however briefly.

There is only the path of this interlacing, the salt on beards,
the shapes of limbs in braided repose, the rise and fall of breath audible in
the whoosh of afternoon, the reeds whispering to the heavens in the ear's
silver screen, the amusement of gulls at the frugality of our tango.
Even if ever we come to fall in the carnival of mirrors,
we will always have had this day.

About the Author

Photo by Mark Rush

Yermiyahu Ahron Taub is the author of three previous books of poetry, *The Insatiable Psalm* (Wind River Press, 2005), *What Stillness Illuminated/ Vos shtilkayt hot baloykhtn* (Parlor Press, 2008; Free Verse Editions series), and *Uncle Feygele* (Plain View Press, 2011). His poems have appeared in numerous journals and anthologies, including *The Prairie Schooner Anthology of Contemporary Jewish American Writing* (University of Nebraska Press, 1998), *Ṭroṭ bay ṭroṭ: hayntṭsayṭike: Yidishe poezye / Step by Step: Contemporary Yiddish Poetry* (Verbarium/Quodlibet, 2009), *Collective Brightness: LGBTIQ Poets on Faith, Religion, and Spirituality* (Sibling Rivalry Press, 2011), and *This Assignment Is So Gay: LGBTIQ Poets on the Art of Teaching* (Sibling Rivalry Press, 2013).

Honored by the Museum of Jewish Heritage as one of New York's Best Emerging Artists, Taub has been nominated twice for a Best of the Net Award and twice for a Pushcart Prize. He lives in Washington, D.C.

Please visit his website at www.yataub.net.

CPSIA information can be obtained at www.ICGtesting.com
Printed in the USA
BVOW08s0145190814

363322BV00002B/20/P